Praise for Natasha Badhwar

'Natasha Badhwar has a rare and beautiful ability to make the personal political, and the political personal. She communicates the wisdom of significant life truths through stories of everyday living.' **Harsh Mander**, human rights and peace worker and author of *Looking Away*, *Fatal Accidents of Birth*, *Ash in the Belly* and others

'The beauty of this book lies in its sentences. They are proof that one can communicate perfectly well without resorting to long-winded sentences. The shallow political dicourse of our times has confused our expressions and articulation. This book shows us how to simplify our language, and ourselves.' **Ravish Kumar**, broadcast journalist, poet and author of *Ishq Mein Shahar Hona* (A City Happens in Love) and *The Free Voice*

'Badhwar rescues relationships and circumstances from their literality to live in the poetic.' **Sumana Roy**, author of *How I Became a Tree and Missing*

'I find Natasha Badhwar's writing insightful and deeply moving for what it reveals about being human. She doesn't look at parenthood or herself through a glossy filter, but with unflinching honesty.' **Amit Varma**, columnist and host of the podcast, *The Seen and the Unseen*

'Badhwar unfurls a gamut of emotions, allows forever to live amongst us an authentic cast of characters and voices; the little people in her world are discovering, growing, watching as we learn to unlearn our bulky, cumbrous ways. I think a reader will be forever grateful to Badhwar and them for giving us permission to unlearn, stumble, be bored, hungry, sulk, play hookey, eat ice cream.' **Aneela Zeb Babar**, author of *We are All Revolutionaries Here*

'The author writes with such self-reflexive vulnerability that you forget you are reading another person's writing. You feel your heart spill out on the page. Through tears and smiles, and a heaving and sinking heart the book embraces the reader, cleansing many heartaches and allowing one to celebrate unspoken joys. You recognise memories you had dumped away, you reclaim parts you had been too ashamed to include in your narrative of self.' **Kiranjeet Chaturvedi**, *Huffington Post*

'Her prose is lucid and heartfelt, and her voice, soothing and warm.' *The Times Of India*

'In her words, you will find comfort for your parenting fears and courage to override the beliefs that you've internalised while growing up. Her writing is raw, honest and relatable.' *Hindustan Times*

'Badhwar's interests are eclectic: to reclaim the inner artist, to break down hierarchies, to occasionally get away with broken grammar.' **Tishani Doshi**, *The Hindu*

'...story that doesn't shy away from the rifts, the tantrums, the silences, and the time it takes to learn how to be better at relationships. This is a complex, loving portrait of a family where it sometimes takes decades to give and to be able to accept the apologies, the explanations, and the peace that one has waited desperately for.' **Urvashi Bahuguna**, *Scroll.in*

'This sense of putting your heart out there and knowing that it is okay to do so filled me with awe. I am in awe of her because she shows her deepest scars, her fears and knows that that is the only way she can connect and know people better.' **Vivek Tejuja**, *The Hungry Reader*

'There is a Natasha in you, me and every woman listening to her heart's voice and trying to make a change to her immediate and not so immediate world. Read it to heal yourself, to feel more confident and open to sharing what you feel in this journey as a feminist, a career woman, an ambitious spouse and a vulnerable mother.' **Anjali G Sharma**, *Women's Web*

Immortal for a Moment

Natasha Badhwar

SIMON & SCHUSTER

London · New York · Sydney · Toronto · New Delhi

First published in India by Simon & Schuster India, 2018

3 5 7 9 10 8 6 4

Simon & Schuster India
818, Indraprakash Building,
21, Barakhamba Road,
New Delhi 110001

www.simonandschuster.co.in

PB ISBN: 978-93-86797-28-5
eBook ISBN: 978-93-86797-29-2

Grateful acknowledgement is made to *Mint Lounge* which publishes the author's column. Other chapters have first appeared in *Outlook*, *NewsCentral24x7.com* and *The Globe and Mail*.

Typeset in India by SÜRYA, New Delhi

Printed and bound in India by Replika Press Pvt. Ltd.

For my parents,
Trilok and Sudha,
and my brothers, Nitish and Manish.
I am because you are.

There's no life
that couldn't be immortal
if only for a moment.

Death
always arrives by that very moment too late.

In vain it tugs at the knob
of the invisible door.
As far as you've come
can't be undone.

Wislawa Szymborska

(Translated by Stanislaw Baranczak & Clare Cavanagh)

Contents

Neither of us knew how to be married

Neither of us knew how to be married. This was not dangerous in itself, although it did get us into many awkward situations. Left to ourselves, of course, we found it hilarious. Early in our marriage we would play house-house as if it were a children's game in which we sometimes got to act like grown-ups. This is what saved us eventually.

To be honest, neither of us wanted to get married either. But again, it was awkward spending so much time in each other's homes and trying to keep our parents convinced that we were really just hanging out innocently.

We were a little weird with each other too. He wasn't a boyfriend-type, though I must admit I was a real perfect girlfriend. On the other hand, when we did get married, I had no intentions of being anyone's wife.

Before we were married, we would "break up" with each other regularly and repeatedly and I would always assume it was the end. I'd feel sick and shattered and prepare to mope around for a while, watching too much television sitting too close to the screen and taking on so much work that I would crash with exhaustion.

He would usually call me in a day or two and try to set up our next date.

'We can't meet,' I'd remind him.

'I am coming towards your office in the evening. What time will you be free?' he'd ask.

'We have broken up,' I would remind him, trying to not let my voice break.

But he wouldn't get it. 'What does that have to do with meeting today,' he'd ask, as if I was being completely illogical. 'Just because we have broken up, doesn't mean we can't meet and talk.'

And we would meet. Or text. Or e-mail. Or chat online. During one of the break ups, I turned up at his home in a village in east Uttar Pradesh with my news television crew. His mother hosted us and extended family members took us around, helping us get interviews and shots for a report on the upcoming elections. He and I sat up late admiring the moon from the inner courtyard till Ammi got out of her bed to ask us to go to our rooms and sleep.

We changed cities to get over each other. I went to Bhilai on a sabbatical from my TV job to teach a media course. He went to Bangalore to work for an IT startup. He got a work visa and accepted a job in Chicago.

True to form, he turned up in Bhilai to visit me when I was there. He was travelling from Morbi in Gujarat to Delhi and told me that he was coming to visit me because Chhattisgarh was on the way. My students and colleagues gave him a hero's welcome even though they had never heard of him before. He bought me a silk saree from Bangalore. I helped him shop for Levi's jeans and new shirts before he left for USA. He turned up at my documentary shoot again when I was in London a few weeks later, carrying heavy equipment and nursing my broken heart. He helped us carry our tripod and light kit all over the city. My colleagues loved him, of course.

I learnt something from the break ups. Because they seemed so final to me, and because each time I would decide to end the love affair with more firmness and determination, I got to experience how I really felt with and without him. I got to taste misery on both sides of the border of love.

I found out that he expressed love differently and he experienced the loss of love differently too. I did not know that this would remain a constant in our lives. I still expect that one day we will align on these parameters.

Aren't we all a little crazy? I know you are shaking your head and saying, 'Yes, but not as much as you.'

Trying to make love work is a crazy idea. It is a useless as well as an essential pursuit. Meanwhile, the rest of our life is always there to distract us when the difficulty level of love seems to overwhelm us. This works the other way round also. We thank our stars for the pockets of love and calm we can retreat to when the complexity of life exhausts us.

'Will you marry me?'

We kept proposing to each other unexpectedly for years after we were finally married. And had children. And had been "accepted" by all the layers of aunts and uncles who had been left out of the decision making process when we had officially got married.

Popping the question every now and then is cute, but as everyone knows, it is best to time it when the answer is likely to be close to the one we are hoping for. In our case, asking each other once again if "*you will marry me*" is a way of reiterating that all said and done, "*I still want to marry you.*"

Sometimes it's a way to ask if we are finally ready to be married-married. Like seriously married. Like proper husband and wife. As if, if we lie low when it gets stormy and stay patient, there is really an ideal that exists for us to arrive at.

Irrespective of dreamy aspirations, it is often an effective strategy to lie low and stay patient in life. It's a great place to get rest. Make resolutions. Meet others and rediscover the first flush of new love. Make friends with one's own self all over again.

Sixteen years later, we continue to misunderstand each other in rather silly ways. Sometimes I say something romantic and still get very unexpected results in response. 'I'm not responsible for taking care of the psychological vacuum in your head,' he said to me the other day and I was like, 'Hey, hello, I was just trying to flirt with you.'

At other times, he will try a clever trick hoping to charm me but I will jump out of my skin and deliver a lecture recounting my unhealed traumas and other childhood anecdotes.

Then there are our children. Marriage doesn't need children to survive. And vice versa. Sometimes a marriage deserves to be demolished for the sake of the children.

I know that I needed my children. I was too vulnerable

without them. I began to build myself up in the way we all deserved when I became their mother. When this new love visited me. Theirs and mine.

Like most other institutions, the template of marriage is dangerously outdated. Men, women and children want to be fuller, more flexible versions of themselves. We want to claim personal autonomy. We want our needs to be respected. Our personal growth will not be postponed interminably. It has pushed its way through the hierarchy of urgencies.

Then there's always travel. When we don't know how to find peace with each other, or peace from others, we leave home to travel. It always helps to disentangle and reset our boundaries.

We spend our lives looking to find our way back to the homes we are fleeing from. Once there was safety in breaking away. When we are stronger, we need closure. Reconciliation.

The great journey of life is to trace the route that takes us back to where we had started from.

I

Right in the Beginning

Just because I make it look easy, doesn't mean it is not difficult.

1

The moments will become stories

It was a Sunday morning. Drizzle resting on still leaves, newspapers rescued from the vegetable patch in the garden. That precious light when I gaze lovingly at this beautiful man who has just dragged a rag doll of me out of bed. Too early. And put a cup of tea in my hands. Urgently.

Sunflowers wave at me from behind the boundary wall. Birds shake off rain.

Any minute now the children will come down the stairs and want to dip Marie biscuits in this romantic moment. This threat of assault adds a thrill. I hold my cup tighter, gripping it with both hands. I need a clever plan to make him put down the newspaper.

My phone beeps a notification. It's usually the bank or the Sauna Slim Belt people at this early hour. Still, I check.

It is Priya Ramani, the editor of *Mint Lounge*. 'Can you start a parenting column this week? Send first piece by Tuesday.'

'Oh sure,' I type back. 'Fabulous.' I put down my phone.

Then I start to cry. Loudly. What have I done? Oh my God.

It works. The beautiful man puts down the newspaper slowly.

Panic. Parenting column. I have said yes. That means I will have to be a good parent. How can I write good things without doing them first?

I will have to be a good person. Live my life more fully. It is so much easier to be an okay-okay person. I will have to play more, talk more, travel more, laugh more. Be more present than absent. Go to children's parks. I might enjoy it eventually, but living life more fully seems like harder work than not.

'Finish your tea. Calm down,' he says, folding the newspaper. I like being told to calm down. It calms me down.

By now, I have also run out of reasons to panic. Now the pluses start trooping in. And so do our children, all three of them.

'I will set myself up for criticism,' I think, adjusting an eight-year-old in my lap. I'm not sure why this is a good thing but it feels like it is. Criticism is for important people. Criticism is childhood. It can bring out the brave in you. It can help you clear the clutter and defend your choices.

'Listen to the kids. They know,' I will write. I will have to listen to my children first. I wrap my free arm around our six-year-old, my head nestling against her. She peers into the teacup in my other hand. Pink nightgowns. Droopy ponytails from yesterday's adventures.

I will tell stories from the moments. The moments will become stories. Now baby is here. She is going to be three years old soon. She scrunches her face and makes a noise. 'Get out of here, you two, this is MY mamma,' she seems to be saying.

'Okay, okay,' the elder sisters go to their father. His lap is bigger. Baby clambers on to me. 'Give me milk,' she gestures, touching my face. 'And all your attention. You are mine. For now.'

I will need more alone time to get any decent writing done. Maybe I can cheat and steal more alone time for myself than one column needs. This is getting more win-win by the minute.

By now, our teatime is over and the children are fully charged.

'What are we going to do today?' asks Sahar.

'We are going to celebrate today,' I say.

'Oh,' she says. 'What are we going to celebrate?'

'We are going to celebrate what a wonderful family we are,' I say to her. I am a bit corny sometimes, but I like to keep it simple.

'Oh,' she says.

Tell me if this makes sense to you. The most important work any of us will ever do is at home, within the oasis of our family and relationships. This is not even work, is it? It is everyday life. Yet this is where our children will get their sense of belonging, security and tolerance. This is where our children will learn how to stand up to injustices and negotiate with differences. This is where we heal our own wounds.

A holiday morning is as good a time as any to make the children feel important. A good time to let one's own inner child run free. There will be conflict and mayhem. There may be joy and peace.

I'll take my chances.

2

Run daughter run

Remember that early 1990s film *Dil Hai Ki Manta Nahin*? Pooja Bhatt's fabulous big hair and the boyish, lean Aamir Khan. In the climax of the film, Anupam Kher walks with his daughter, Pooja, towards the *mandap* where her groom waits to marry her. Throughout the walk, he tries to convince his daughter to run away right then and chase her lover, played by Khan. He will love her better, and truer.

There is a white Maruti van he has arranged for the runaway bride.

'*Bhaag jaa, beti, bhaag jaa*,' he says, almost begging her. 'Run, daughter, run.'

As parents of little daughters, Afzal and I sometimes indulge in idle conversation about how they might get married one day. He openly expresses violent feelings towards potential lovers. I like to think that I will be like Seth Dharamchand, the eccentric, liberated parent Kher plays in *Dil Hai Ki Manta Nahin*.

'Run, daughter, run. Be impulsive. Follow your heart. Make it big.'

Well, this is how my performance went on the first day our youngest daughter started school and it was time for me to get my first dose of separation from her.

Naseem ran to the bus stop. She hopped, skipped and jumped. She sang. She got on a bus for the first time in her life. By the time she sat in her seat, she no longer had a view or a sense of direction of which side we were standing. She waved randomly. The bus took her away.

Seth Dharamchand be damned. I must go after my daughter.

'I'm going to sit in the school reception and work on my laptop,' I say to Afzal.

'It will be better for you to stay at home,' he says.

'But it will be so peaceful, no? I can concentrate better and write there.'

He gives me the look. 'Go to your Dosa Corner. Or the coffee shop,' he says. 'Very peaceful, this early in the morning.'

'There's such a nice aquarium in the school,' I say. 'Big glittering fish in it. I will write well there.'

Another look.

'Okay. I'll complain about you in my next column,' I say to him. I'm feeling desperate. Very desperate.

'So what,' he says, 'I'm not afraid of looking like a fool. That's your problem.'

I don't know how he knows, but that is exactly what my problem is. The fear of looking foolish. The fear of being told not to be silly.

I have been typing and un-typing my feelings about seeing my youngest child become independent of me for days now. Words have failed me. I have failed my words.

There is a tightness in my throat. As if someone is gripping it and not letting a coherent voice speak up. That someone is also me. 'What's the big deal, Natasha? Little children start school all the time,' says the strict voice of reason in my head.

This voice, however, doesn't sound reasonable at all. It sounds condescending to me.

These are feelings, man. Feelings must be felt. And expressed. It leads to better productivity. It unleashes creativity. It protects the ozone layer. And ultimately contributes to better sex lives.

Just because I feel like crying, does not mean I am unhappy. Just because I care for the details, does not mean I have gone to pieces. Just because I am jittery, does not mean I am not prepared.

Coming together with each other, then going our own separate ways. Getting on top of things, then plummeting at top speed. Figuring it out, then forgetting again. Not always getting it, but being determined to deal with it.

It's a lovely loop really. Life is never a straight road.

Meanwhile, the first day of school is almost over. I'm back at the bus stop to receive my baby. The baby who is not a baby any more. It is a sunny winter afternoon and everything seems all right from this angle. Just that I feel like something has been yanked out of me.

Here comes the yellow bus.

3

Why was this time so difficult?

My brain is saying go to sleep,' says Naseem, 'but my heart wants to do colouring.'

'Whaaaa,' I say. 'Can you say that again?'

'My heart is not listening to my brain. It wants to do colouring.'

It is late at night. We are speaking in whispers. I have just settled on the floor with my laptop, after the family had gone to sleep around me. Naseem is three years old, our youngest child. She has climbed out of bed to share her inner conflict with me. We need to address it.

We get a box of crayons and a white sheet of paper. We settle down again. Naseem draws circles and lines. She chooses her colours. Artists must listen to their heart. Particularly when they are in the middle of summer vacation.

I feel tired. My feet hurt. I fall off to sleep at unlikely hours, in unexpected places. Holding my bag like a pillow in my lap, snug in the women's compartment of the Delhi Metro. Sitting with my eyes shut, in the dentist's waiting room, to avoid watching the evening news on the wall-mounted TV. Someone nudges me awake. I think it's your turn.

'You do too much,' my mother often says. 'Get some rest. Learn to say no to some things. Send the children to me for a couple of days.'

'You do too little,' says the voice in my head. 'You are lazy and inefficient.' This voice also sounds uncannily like that of my parents. Now playing in a loop inside me.

Growing up means listening to everyone. Growing up means listening to everyone and then not listening to anyone. Let your sleep catch up with you wherever it finds you. Sometimes I wake up with my jaw drooping. Fix the jaw, laugh at yourself and gather your wits again. Smile at strangers. You're a grown-up. It's safe.

My husband leans over my shoulder to read as I type.

'Go away,' I say, putting the screen down.

'Why, why, why?' he says.

'Please, I just started writing,' I say. 'It's terrible right now, like vomit.'

'So,' he says, smiling. 'You're talking as if I haven't seen your vomit before.'

Oh well. A rush of memories distracts me. Love is remembering the times you threw up on your lover. Love is letting him read your first draft. Hoping his phone will ring and take him away.

Naseem and I are sitting at the dining table. It is past

three in the afternoon. The older children have settled with their books in cool corners of the home. Naseem didn't eat lunch with the rest of us. She demands her own rhythm and by now the parent in me is both patient enough and too tired to resist. It's the youngest child syndrome. I have realised that all the hard work that has gone into the fixing, moulding and reshaping of the older children has not been a favour to them.

'Mama, why do you scold me?' Naseem says. Her mouth shaped like a baby bird.

'I scold you?' I say.

'Oho, don't you scold me sometimes?' she says.

'When?'

'When I do bad things.'

'You do bad things?' I say, my eyes doing most of the talking.

'Yes. When I beat my sisters, remember?'

'You beat your sisters?' I say, looking mildly horrified.

'Yes, don't you know, I wear my chappals in my hands and run after them.'

'Really?' I say.

'Yes.' She laughs. She is looking embarrassed now. 'Then you scold me.'

'Should I not scold you then?' I say.

'You should,' she says. She goes back to finishing her lunch.

Sometimes it startles me, how each child has brought out a completely different parent in us. This is the first summer vacation when our children are not dependant on me so much. I can depend on them. I'm sure they feel I have grown up too. When an afternoon lasts too long, as summer afternoons do, I crawl into their circle and curl up into a nap.

I don't call them power naps any more. I power down.

Why was this time so difficult? Why did we grouse, moan, whine, whimper so much? When I look back later, I may not remember. Or maybe there will be shining clarity. Recovery is not a full stop. We are always recovering.

We are in the car, driving to my parents' home. Old Hindi film songs are playing on the car stereo. Naseem is sitting in my lap.

'When I grow up, Mamma, I will read your articles,' she says, turning to look at me.

'Whaaaa,' I say. All over again.

On both sides of the road, summer trees, their branches flushed with flowers, rush past us.

4

Unnecessary happiness. Why are you so happy?

I burnt the onions accidentally.

There they were, cut really small, dancing and sizzling in hot oil. Two omelettes had already been received at the dining table with whoops of delight.

I was whipping eggs with a fork for the third when my mind wandered away from where I was.

Words rushed in anxiously. But the onions in the pan burnt themselves.

Our first born, Sahar, was nine that year. She was on her way to Amritsar in a train. In a Shatabdi, which is the best kind of train in Sahar's imagination. 'It's even better than aeroplanes, Mamma,' she says, fantasizing about the tetra pack juice, ketchup sachets, bread sticks and butter chiplets. You cannot even imagine what all else. Ice cream too.

Five teachers and 60 children have gone on a school

trip, and our daughter is one of the youngest in the group. When Sahar first came home with the details of the trip, the decision had came instantly to me. 'Of course, you can go, darling. You must go.' We are travellers by nature. Born to explore.

When it was time to pack, suddenly I remember that Sahar is only nine years old.

Is nine old enough?

I mean she's really eight and a half. I wish I had known there would be no turning back. How could I not have known?

Just then, Afzal called out to say that tea was ready.

'I'm going to have a panic attack,' I said to him.

He looked at me.

I closed my eyes. Tears rolled. I thought of my Mum.

I can see that Afzal is struggling with something but he is not going to talk about it. The tea is good. I wipe my cheeks and dip biscuits.

I have given my best backpack to Sahar. I have emptied out my own toilet bag to keep her clips and her inhaler. I notice how together we are as we pack. She isn't asking for Dora or Barbie stamped accessories. She has loads of them to choose from, but fashion is not on her mind right now. I am surprised. And impressed.

At school, the children have been shown video clips of the change of guard at Wagah, the border between India and Pakistan. Sahar is showing Aliza how high the soldiers raise their legs. Little Naseem laughs at their performance.

I remember the first day we had sent Sahar to playschool.

One part of me had been so wound up about it that I had taken a whole week off from work. The school was 2 minutes from home and an hour's drive from my office.

I had reached school 40 minutes in advance to pick her up. Drawn like a magnet, I sat in the lobby, clutching my unsuccessful Sudoku and pen.

Then the children started walking out one by one, led to the school bus waiting for them.

The teacher saw me and indicated that she would bring Sahar out soon. I was chatting with other children near me, being funny in a way that caused some of them to wrap themselves around their parent's legs. Others to come closer to me for a better view.

After 10 minutes of all this, Sahar appeared.

My three-year-old daughter's face in the doorway in a group of other children. She looked at me. We yelled with joy. We hugged, and laughed and slapped each other happily.

Unnecessary happiness. That's the term that had come to my intellectual, literary head. Why are you so happy?

Shut up, brain! My heart had replied, rather inarticulately.

Half a decade later, I had a better answer. I knew the answer. I am happy because I am ready to let her go. I am happy because she will be back. We are ready to separate, because we belong together.

I think of our child napping in her inclined seat on the train right now. Sunny fields outside her window. A little bit of me has gone with her. That bit which keeps her safe and keeps me reassured.

Amritsar is my mother's hometown. My grandmother

used to start her day with a visit to the Harmandir Sahib. In my mind, I see my daughter walking on the stone floors that had given solace to her grandmother and great-grandmother. Sahar is visiting her own history. When she returns home, I might show her these words. She will read this aloud, slowly like a nine-year-old.

I will feel unnecessarily happy all over again, as if all the pieces of a jigsaw puzzle have come together

5

Are sisters the perfect best friends?

One evening, Naseem, the youngest of the three sisters discovered a playful use for the black computer cover of my laptop. While her two sisters were immersed in their never-ending daily homework, Naseem stuck two large circular paper eyes on either side of the cover and attached a conical horn to one of its corners. Then she unzipped the rectangular cover and wore it over her head, so that the horn seemed to stick out from her forehead. She had become a unicorn.

She practised her act on me first, and being her parent, I was happy to see her as whatever she was imagining herself as. I squealed with delight and admired her wobbly horse-like dance. She went up to her sisters' room to get a few startled laughs from them. She had less success than she was expecting. One ignored her, the other was irritable.

'Mamma, these guys are so rude to me,' she said to me, her unicorn head now looking sad. 'They are mean.'

'It's okay, *beta*,' I consoled her. 'They are your sisters. It's their job to be rude.'

I grew up without sisters. My relationship with my two brothers was colourful and privileged, yet for some reason I remember always pining for a sister. My mother is one of six sisters. Most of my friends in my all-girls' school in Kolkata seemed to have lots of sisters. I hoped for some of this intangible magic in my life. I wanted a girl in my life. Female energy.

Decades later, as our three daughters laugh, talk and sing together, I listen with an unadulterated sense of awe. Often I feel like I'm a spectator on a film set, watching them effortlessly create scenes together. I write down dialogues I overhear, so I can replay them years later.

I have been wanting to write about being sisters for a while now. I am acutely conscious of the fact that I know very little about this. I really have no insider's experience.

One of the definitions of sisterhood that has stayed with me was provided by our second child, Aliza, when she was still a toddler. She entered my room and found me wearing my husband's T-shirt.

'This is Papa's T-shirt,' she said.

'Yes, it is,' I said.

'Are you two sisters?' she said.

'Whaaaa?' I must have gone in my head. Then I realized that little Aliza had interpreted from her life experiences that sisters are those who are forced to share each others' clothes, toys and room.

A decade later, Aliza can expand on that definition.

As she peers at this laptop screen to see me writing about sisters, she helpfully offers some quotes.

'Mamma, sometimes I hate them. Sometimes I love them also. Sometimes I kill them.'

I look up at her. 'In my head,' she adds. 'But then I think to myself, if they weren't here, I would be a brat.'

I'm glad she has a generous reason to spare the life of her sisters.

Our older daughters, Sahar and Aliza, are slightly less than two years apart in age. People often ask if they are twins. Sometimes they are too close to each other for their own comfort. The youngest, Naseem, arrived late to the party and has to rely on ingenious ways to be included.

I walked into a mini-disaster zone one time. Aliza was playing by herself and had created an elaborate set where a family of small wooden dolls were leading their lives amidst miniature lifestyle props like a flat screen television, comfortable sofas, bookshelves and lamps. I don't know what followed what, but by the time I reached the scene, catastrophe had struck, the dolls were scattered and there were dark clouds of anger and gloom hovering over the two sisters.

Thankfully, I have learnt by now that it isn't my role to try to dispense justice. I sat down at a safe distance. After a while I spoke to Naseem, who was sitting by herself on the stairs.

'Are you feeling guilty about destroying Aliza's family?' I asked.

'No, Mamma, she said. 'I just feel alone.'

Denial kicked in almost immediately. She couldn't have used that word. How can a child who has never been alone, feel alone?

She did. It is the nature of all love relationships to make you experience extreme emotions. I remember thinking that one advantage of dividing the world into countries with borders is that it is an effective way to separate warring siblings. Bhai and I get along so well now, after we have been safely separated by continents. Perhaps that's how it all started, this business of visas and restricted entries to other people's territories.

Ever since we have become a family of three daughters, we observe others who are a similar combination of siblings. I make notes. I am always delighted and reassured to meet others who are also sisters. I notice this detail in friends and family that I have always known. I want to hear their stories. I watch them like a student on assignment.

I pay attention to how sisters support each other. How they survive and flourish despite the cruel comparisons, the competition, and the meagreness of resources—both emotional and physical. How they challenge the pressure to be nothing more than pretty and obedient. How they defy low expectations to restore their original selves. How they rally behind each other again and again.

'Will you all look out for each other when I am gone?' I sometimes ask my children blatantly and seemingly out of the blue.

'Yes, Mamma,' they chorus in response. They are used to me by now.

6

Brothers and sisters—No strings attached

I have two brothers. Bhai, who is older, is the novel I might write one day. Manu, our funny-serious kid brother, is my collection of short stories.

I love my brothers. They are tall and funny. Either they are making the rest of us laugh, or are happy to let us laugh at them. In a way they are the story of my life.

Despite this, every year when Raksha Bandhan—the festival that celebrates the love of sisters for their brothers—comes around, I just want to ignore it and look the other way till it has passed. I feel like the ritual of Rakhi comes between my brothers and me.

I look back at us and see the three of us wrestling, playing, cycling, recording song compilations, writing slogans for TV contests, collecting data in our quiz notebook and teasing each other with burp and fart jokes. Scaring each other with ghost stories.

Bhai was the leader of our pack with his magic shows, his science project expertise, his imitation of Abdul Qadir's bowling style and his re-telling of Shakespeare's plays on our way to and from the milk booth everyday. Manu was forever in motion, his skateboard whizzing through the length of our home on endless summer afternoons. He gave me hockey and football lessons on the roof, so that he could have an opponent to play against. He obediently played badminton with me when it was prescribed as physiotherapy for my broken elbow, all stiff and clumsy as it emerged from its cast.

On Rakhi morning, suddenly we would find ourselves separated into brothers and sister. The boys and the girl. Family, culture and society would step in with a different sort of narrative. Stories of helpless women in trouble. Their brothers, real and imagined, expected to rescue them from being dishonoured. The generosity of brothers and the giggly gratitude of sisters. The reminder that the sister is vulnerable and the brother invincible. The announcement of the 'auspicious' time. As we became young adults, Raksha Bandhan began to leave me cold. I really didn't need it.

Manu finished school and went to a regional engineering college in Jamshedpur. He didn't want to be an engineer. When he returned home two months later, his lips were swollen and his face marked by the slaps and blows that had been part of routine ragging in his college. He didn't want to go back, but he had to. The next time he returned, he told me ugly stories of caste politics and student violence deep into the night.

The third time he returned in the same year, Manu was adamant that he was never going back.

'It's teething troubles,' I tried to convince him. 'You'll find a way to make a space for yourself.'

'You have no idea,' he said. 'The way these boys talk about girls, the way they harass them in markets and cinema halls...I cannot stay in that place, leave alone study there. I will go mad.'

That was a Raksha Bandhan moment for me. I knew I had to stand by my brother now. He needed me to protect him, to support him to protect himself. We negotiated with our parents. Manu never went back.

A few years later, I was in a hotel room in Kemps Corner, Bombay, when the phone rang. Bhai was calling from New York. He had fallen in love and he wanted her to know his family. He was asking me to write a letter to someone I had never met. For him. That day was Raksha Bandhan for Bhai and me.

I have value for tradition that binds. That underlines how we are equals despite differences. Not one that imposes roles and choices that feel blatantly false, that don't fit the reality of our lives.

I own my relationship with my brothers. It is the purest thing in my life. Underneath the obvious one, is a secret bond. We know stories that were never told. We have seen pain that was never expressed. We are oral historians of each others' lives. We will always be there for each other, irrespective of whether the online Rakhi store delivers on time or not, unconditional of whether I turn up at Manu's office lobby to tie a Rakhi on his wrist or not.

Every time one of us calls the other on the long drive to

work, it is Raksha Bandhan. Every time we don't bother to buy each other gifts because love is all we need, it is Rakhi. Every time we look at each other's children and want to squeeze them tight because they remind us of us, it is Rakhi.

All sisters are extraordinarily protective of their brothers. We need a festival that honours that too. When I pick up the three grains of rice soaked in red and put that tilak on my brother's forehead on the day of the festival, the thought in my mind is, 'Go on Bhai, be the best version of yourself, I am here to protect you. To hold you.'

II

Marriage, Don't Do It

Marriage is what begins to work when you begin to give up on it.

7

Love is vulnerable. It doesn't know its way home

One evening we lost our two-year-old in the park.

We had just moved into a new home. There were unexpected guests and a pocket of chaos as we cleared away cartons on the floor and put enough chairs for everyone. Cool water and sweets were offered. Pleasantries.

Our children were playing outside. Aliza, our five-year-old, came running in to let us know that she couldn't find Naseem any more.

My first reaction in an emergency is to stay calm. I ran out with Aliza to the forest park next to our new home. Too many people, gates, trees, bushes, a pond. It was a large space. I was not wearing my spectacles.

How long was it that I was alone in that barrenness? 10, 5, 20 minutes? Some people said they had seen her, some stared at me blankly. Everyone was a stranger. I sent Aliza to call her father.

'Tell him that I cannot find Naseem, run and get Papa,' I said to her.

By now, my world had begun to whirl around me. It was Afzal's turn to be calm. When he found our child, she was sitting near a faraway gate with a flower in her hand.

'I got this for Mamma,' she said.

This month we complete 10 years of being married to each other. It seems like a good time to revisit the moment when I was ready to run out of our home without looking back.

That time when I had been standing in the park paralysed by fear, unable to find our toddler, the thought in my head had been: If anything happens to Naseem, I will leave Afzal.

Later that evening, after I had finished crying, put Naseem to sleep and worn her flower in my hair, I was left with the residue of my panicked thoughts. I had not known that I was this close to the edge in my head.

'I don't know who or what this marriage is but it better not come between my wife and me,' a friend had once written to me.

Marriage is an accident-prone adventure. It gets hijacked, kidnapped, derailed, distracted and exhausted. Marriage can become a pile of resentments.

Togetherness is a venue. We seek it for respite. For nurturing and rest. We go there to practise fighting. It's a boxing ring. Boxing is a sport, remember. We play at boxing to be better prepared for the rest of the world. We analyse our strengths, compensate for weaknesses.

But don't always stay there. Go away also. Be independent.

Don't expect it to work all the time. It is lazy and busy and easily distracted. Just like the lovers in it.

And then there are children. Children are like a JCB machine. They will wreck your marriage and play with the debris. If they don't come along and create utter chaos, something else always does. If nothing else shakes us up, it is quite likely that we will start feeling itchy and draw blood ourselves.

Marriage isn't necessary at all. Don't do it. It's a lot of trouble. It's a racket. A conspiracy to defeat the individual. A human rights violation that creeps up on you.

Marriage can be lonesome. Being together won't stop you from being alone, lost, tempted, greedy, insecure and sleepless.

Just like a two-year-old playing outside the house, love is vulnerable. It is gentle and happy. It can be wild and tantrum-prone. It doesn't know its way home.

Love learns to walk. It takes years to grow up. Be gentle with it, holding its hand when the traffic is fast.

Love is looking at him in the evening light and being able to smell the tea that you will have with him. Even on a train. Specially on a train.

Love is made of still images. Clothes hanging together on a clothes peg in the bathroom. Messages saved in an inbox. Earrings next to a black leather wallet. A mole on the back. A shared backpack.

Love sulks for attention. Sometimes you make up because there's a rat behind the washing machine and you need company to deal with it. Sometimes the rat is just an excuse.

Love gets taken for granted. We forget what it was like in the first place.

'Come and help me choose my shirt,' he says.

'I am working,' I say.

'Please, I have no idea what to wear today.'

'Is that your way of saying you love me?'

'You're the expert,' he says.

Be creative. Have an affair with the one you love, so what if you are also married to each other. That's one way to subvert this system.

Falling in love with the same silly smile again and again and again. That's *shaadi* for you. Total *barbaadi*. Don't do it. Seriously.

8

A welcome note for new husbands and wives

Do not be in a hurry to become one of these—a husband or a wife. Take your time. Change your mind many times. Be suspicious of prefabricated labels and roles. Be prepared to be inventive.

Even when you do get married, do not go running towards the quicksand. Slow down, amble around, check out the new terrain at your own pace. Participate in the costume drama that Indian marriages are, but see yourself as an intern. Be a part-timer in the beginning, if you need to. Hold on to all your other commitments and loves. Love more than just people.

All of us are surrounded by others who believe that they know better than us how we must conduct ourselves as husbands and wives. It is easier to be invested in other people's lives. It is more entertaining too. Look at them with the blank expression of someone who speaks a different language. Say something inappropriate or awkward once in a while to distract them.

Marriage has a sense of entitlement, it demands a lot of space, time and energy. It wants to be centre of stage all the time. Do not grant permission. Treat it politely as if it were a stranger. Take some time for the ice to break.

Some marriages are aloof. Some are absent even when the curtains have lifted and the stage has been set. Collect the clues as they present themselves.

Many of us have spent too much time imagining what our marriage will be like. We have a template ready. Templates have limited use. They become obsolete and must be discarded.

Men, fall in love with smart women if that rocks your boat. Fall in love with someone who is self-contained. Marry her. Don't accuse her of being too smart afterwards. Make space for smartness.

Women, fall in love with tender men. Marry one of them. Don't abandon his vulnerability when he becomes your husband. Don't be embarrassed by it. Protect him.

Indifference is an important part of love. True love hurts. It gnashes, bites, tramples and sits on you. It is mean. It transfers all its baggage on to you and accuses you of being the baggage. You will learn to shield yourself. You cannot let the hurt reach you each time it is unleashed. You will create pockets of indifference, so that you can remain you.

It's a shock when we manage to do this for the first time. You expect that your love will surround you and keep you perpetually covered in its gentle drizzle. Or its downpour. You will step away. You will want to get away. You must.

Love tires. It needs rest. It hibernates.

Marriage is a series of disagreements. First you will learn how to stand up to each other. You will discover how to really get to each other. Then you will learn to back off from arguments sooner. You will teach yourself to let go of the temptation to fire clever one-liners when there is no time or energy to collect and clean up the debris created by the targeted drones that are your words.

Sooner or later, marriage will make you feel incompetent and unskilled. You will be disappointed with this development. After some wallowing, you are ready for the next step. It's not your spouse, it's you.

She is not making you feel small. You are making yourself feel small. He is not pushing you into a corner. You can walk out of there. She is not ignoring you and he is not being callous—you can ask for help, you can give instructions, you can get the attention you need.

Be prepared for the unexpected. You will expect to hate the other's absence. You might even be clingy. Then you will cross a threshold and find that you crave the dreamy, lavender-scented solitude you can surround yourself with when your spouse is away.

You might become jealous of your own child because the other parent is tender and relaxed with the infant but disgruntled and exhausted with you. Don't try to be more like the baby, it won't yield the results you expect.

Most marriages are a collection of dissimilitudes of mind

and etiquette. You will celebrate and mourn differently, you will feel and express love, gratitude, pain, hunger, lust, anger and humour differently. Sometimes marriage is home, sometimes it will strand you on a planet of aliens.

Dear new husbands and wives, marriage is what begins to work when you begin to give up on it. Lower your expectations, as the great elders have always said. Just smile and wave, especially when you are planning your great comeback. Be sure you are always planning something!

9

When does a marriage really begin to become itself?

I hate attending weddings. They are phony, wasteful and irrelevant affairs and I really don't understand why people work so hard to get rid of their money overnight.

The only wedding I didn't mind so much was my own. It had its moments. My friend Reena was still fixing the last safety pins on my cream and gold dupatta when a couple of grown women barged into the dressing room and enthusiastically addressed me as 'Mami!' Apparently they were thrilled to be my new nieces. The shy, beatific bride face that I had been practising disintegrated in shock. I wasn't yet prepared for the side-effects of marriage.

Many hours later, there was the moment when someone handed me a plateful of biryani and it began to feel like maybe this was going to be worthwhile after all. It turned out to be impossible to put anything other than a few bits of flavoured rice between my lips because of the larger-than-my-cheek nose ring that I had been balancing on my left nostril. My newly minted, sherwani-clad husband helped me eat, and I was relieved to find that underneath the grand costume, it was the same guy after all. Someone took a photo of the moment.

Years later, you can't tell how petrified we both were at that time, as we giggle at each other with a spoonful of biryani balanced between us.

And finally there was my father. All through my childhood, he had created confusion by wiping his own tears at scenes in the movies when a bedecked but distraught bride is separated from the embrace of her helpless parents during the *bidai*—the tearjerking ritual when the bride leaves her parents' home to travel to her husband's parents' home. Now, when it was time for his only daughter to leave the marriage venue, my father decided to look utterly exuberant and fulfilled.

Maybe it was because the wedding was taking place in my friend, Geet's farmhouse and we were all eager to get home anyway. Maybe it was the other unconventional details. I was getting into a car we had borrowed from Geet, and were going to drive across town, drop my new in-laws off at their home and come back to my own apartment in the city. Who knows? I would have appreciated some sombreness from my brother and father, but alas, there was none.

So really, to borrow from a famous proverb, marriage is like a box of chocolates. You never know what you're going to get. Most of us love only one type out of the mixed assortment, and can barely tolerate the rest. Often we read the labels too late and have to smile through the fruits, nuts and dates hidden within the devious packaging. Some of us choose to throw tantrums instead.

The reason I am grumpy about attending weddings is that they seem to have no connection to what marriage is really all about eventually. I am snooty about wedding buffet spreads. The bejewelled outfits make my skin rebel. More importantly, I am impatient for the real thing. When does a marriage really begin to become itself?

Does it start when the festivities are over, the wedding gifts have been put away in lofts, and one walks into the jostle of rush hour traffic to get back to work? Does the transition happen when the bride takes off those identifying red and white plastic bangles that seem to have become so ubiquitous on the wrists of newly married women in north India?

Or does one really arrive when you have your first full-blown fight and feel the whiplash of how badly it throws you off? Is it further down the road, on that morning when you realise with relief that you have slept soundly all night without having bothered to resolve that nasty argument that had shaken the walls of your home the previous night? You're no longer afraid of being abandoned due to a disagreement. You two are in this together.

For some, it feels like a new beginning when the children finally move out of the bedroom. Is this what a real honeymoon is supposed to feel like? Your own bed, in your own home, all to yourself! (This doesn't last, of course. The kids keep returning with some excuse or the other. The last time I moved back into my parents' bedroom was when I was pregnant with my third baby, so it's a long haul, folks.)

Does marriage start when you run out of the youthful enthusiasm of fighting like equals and start faking agreement with each other, just so that the other will leave you alone to do things your own way?

Perhaps now being married can also mean being free, like our parents had promised when they asked us to postpone our right to basic human liberties till we grew up and got married.

My aunt tells me that her marriage to her beloved husband really found its home when their daughters had got married and moved to other countries and her in-laws had passed on. She glows like a bride even as she talks about her knee replacement surgery. 'Your generation has no patience,' she says. I save up the same sentence for the generation after mine. I am prepared to be judged, just as I judge my own aunt.

I have friends who are doing a great job of being married to each other after they have been separated and finally divorced. They share childcare duties, go for family therapy together, and make everyone else jealous of how supportive they are of each other. Their children tell them that they have too much in common.

Their relationship proved to be fragile but their love seems unbreakable. Or is it the other way around? Their love broke, but the relationship endures.

In the beginning, we set too much store by love. We don't

know how to recognise it. Popular culture has deceived us. We betray our own expectations. Nothing seems to work for too long.

Marriage was supposed to be about creating a home, doing smart finances, travelling together, looking good, creating Facebook albums and tweeting secretly, right? Well, I won't say wrong. Its about all this and more. Often it is about less.

The first time I called my therapist for help, she left me with words I struggled to understand. We had moved homes, our children were very young, I was struggling to keep things together at home and work and I called her because I was overwhelmed.

'You have to examine the structure of your marriage,' she said to me.

'It's not about my husband,' I said. 'He is not even here. It's me, I am unable to cope. I feel so confused.'

'Confusion is good,' she had said. 'It's like a fog, stopping you from choosing a path that will lead nowhere. Stop where you are. Perhaps you need to change the design of your life.'

I hadn't thought about the structure of a marriage till then. It hadn't yet occurred to me that there were variations possible in its design. I was still a newbie. It was a surprise to find out that there were various routes that I could choose. I could pause. I didn't have to get stuck every day.

A decade later, if you give me two minutes to talk about marriage and how we can make it work, I have an answer ready. Put the women and the children in the centre of the family circle, I will say. Their presence and their needs have been marginalised for too long. This is the root cause of mental illness, of childhood trauma, of loneliness and isolation within our most intimate spaces. It locks us into the cycle of domination and coercion, as men and women become victims and perpetrators, turn by turn.

A good marriage teaches us a new vocabulary. New ways to behave. To learn to take what we need. It makes activists out of us. Once we begin to see how patriarchal structures and roles undermine our individual growth, we learn to question it in society and culture too. Our survival depends on this.

You know you are in a good marriage if everything and everyone seems to be changing all the time. Change is growth. It needs space. And security.

The timid one becomes ready to grow out into a tigress. The outgoing one wants to reveal his most basic insecurities. Traumas of the past return and demand healing. Our childhood biases return like a security blanket. We didn't sign up for a string of surprises all life long, and yet that's what we find in the fine print that's part of this package deal called marriage.

Marriage isn't just about being parents together. Or about being our inner child together. It is also about learning to become adults. Togetherness is not possible without separateness. Being able to go off on one's own path without fear of repercussions. That is part of the liberty we all need from life. It's the best part in this box of chocolates called marriage.

10

The man who never wanted to be a father

I don't remember exactly what it was that started this conversation. We were out for a walk in a park after dinner. The children were scampering ahead of us.

'I am becoming more and more like a mother and you are becoming like a father these days,' Afzal said to me.

'That sounds like a good thing,' I said.

'I'm not sure it's a good thing,' he said.

'It is, Afzal,' I said. 'One person doing the same thing all the time gets depleted. Like farmers rotate crops, we need to be the other parts of ourselves too. People who don't get a break become angry. And bitter.'

'Like our mothers,' he almost completed my sentence softly.

'Like our fathers too,' I added.

Naseem, the youngest, comes running towards us. Splotch! Her foot lands in a dark patch in the path. She almost bounces out of her sandal, which is stuck in the wet mud. Some giggling, little crying and a treacherous rescue. Also, end of conversation.

Afzal leads the way home, holding Naseem mid-air and at arm's length to avoid getting wet mud on him. I do the same with the 'favourite sandal' that the child is more worried about and follow them with our older children.

I know a man who never wanted to be a father. He is the father of our three children. His daughters have started to become quite bossy with him. Very bossy.

Naseem climbs over him like he is a tree and perches on his shoulders. Next she tries to sit on his head.

'Are you a monkey?' he says.

'Yes. Come and make a puzzle with me,' she answers. She has absolute power over him. 'My Papa,' she asserts.

Sahar, who is eight at the time, scolds him, tells him off, and explains things to him very slowly. Sometimes she interrupts our absent-minded conversations to explain to Afzal what I really mean. Or want.

'Let me speak,' he will say. 'I am explaining something to Natasha.'

She will clamp her hand on his mouth, sealing his lips.

'Am I talking too much?' he will say in a garbled voice from behind her fingers.

'Look how he sounds,' she will announce with glee. The others will mimic him. Like audio playing in rewind mode.

Aliza is our middle child. We used to call Afzal and Aliza twins, when she was a baby. Afzal would stick his stubbly face next to her cheeks and ask: 'Don't we look like twins? Tell, tell.'

Many years ago, we were travelling in a state transport bus on our way from Dharamsala to Pathankot. We had the seats right in front of the bus, on the left of the driver's seat. A fabulous panoramic view, and the soundtrack of enthusiastic honking all the way down from the mountains to the plains. I had my *dupatta* loosely over my head and face to protect it from the heat and dust. And to soften the light, I suspect, so I looked pretty to him.

'Why do you want to marry me?' he asked me.

'I think you will make a good father to my children,' I said.

'I'm quite sure I never want to have children,' he said. I had heard that a few times before.

I've always known that I want to be a parent. Afzal was always clear about not wanting to be one. I have looked back at my growing-up years and said, 'I am going to show you how it is supposed to be done.' Perhaps he looked back at his times and thought, 'Man, what a mess! Why bother at all?'

Sometimes it takes a while to realize that two seemingly opposite positions can actually be motivated by similar experiences. People who express conflicting views may be the perfect allies, with the same goals and aspirations. Our words are often deceptive, and we need to go beyond them to begin to see in our hearts.

I show this to Afzal. 'I have called you a man who never wanted to have any children,' I say to him.

He reads. 'Don't use the past tense,' he laughs. 'I still don't want to have any children.'

'You're so clever, no?' I say.

'I'm just being honest, Natasha. This is scary stuff.'

'Just like the adventures you chase,' I say. 'The demons you like to slay. The rescue missions you paraglide into. The cliffs you'd like to jump off from...'

'Can you give me a new snake and monkey story idea?' he says. 'Naseem is sitting on the pot in the bathroom, waiting for a new story from me, and that's my challenge for now.'

'Oh, you mean, one day at a time, baby?' I say.

'Now that's clever,' he says.

11

Money and marriage—How we learnt to spent and save

'What will you do with all this money you save every month,' Afzal used to ask me regularly. This would usually coincide with me scrutinizing a restaurant bill carefully after we had been on a date together.

'It is for my children's school fees,' I would answer without pause.

It was an exchange that never failed to amuse my husband before we were married. We were both working hard, travelling frequently and always busy—but I was the one who earned a big fat salary for my efforts. He was still seeking, wandering, dabbling. Doing everything that came his way without a worry.

My brother put a finger on this difference between him and me before I did.

'Property,' he said by way of explanation. 'People like

you and me—children of middle-class, salary-dependent families—follow the higher education and stable job route to financial security. Those from the land-owning class make creative, unusual, meandering choices—because they always have a fall-back option.'

When we got married, we discovered that we did have one thing in common. We both disliked talking and worrying about money. Both of us had childhood memories of stress in our families and tension between our parents over money, or the insufficiency of it. In our own home, we were determined to not make money an extra member of the family—the one that couples are always talking about behind its back.

Yet, in practice, it seemed that we had taken lifestyle decisions that seemed to be on opposite sides of the spectrum. I saved, I stashed and spent money very conservatively. He would spend, lose, lend and find other ways to get rid of any money he had. Which was funny till we got married.

Afzal felt my extreme saving ways were neurotic and I was sure that his extravagance was over the top. He didn't seem to value the sense of identity and security I got from my job and I struggled to answer people when I was asked what my husband really does.

We found great solace in shared jokes. While balancing our accounts one day, in our early years, I remarked that if he wound up his business ventures entirely, our net family income would increase. We would save the money he was spending on his commute, office rent and staff salaries.

Since he would be free to drive my car, I could divert the driver's salary to him and we would save even more. Plus we would have more couple-time together.

I'm not sure why he loved this proposition so much, but he hasn't stopped repeating it to a contagion of shocked family elders ever since.

'Natasha says that if I shut down my start-ups and start driving her car instead, we will be better off financially.'

To be honest, I thoroughly enjoyed the fruits of his extravagant plans—the holidays abroad, the furniture shopping and the building of our home in our 30s. I learnt to spend money on myself to keep up with him. It felt good.

I also learnt to hide my money from him in envelopes stashed between clothes. It was the only money we lost when our home was burgled. It didn't feel so good.

It was a teachable moment. Why had we begun to keep things from each other, any way? It was okay to not be convinced by the other's rationale. I didn't have to pretend to agree with him and then feel that I had to cover the tracks of my real decisions.

Thankfully we had children really quickly. We were distracted from each other soon enough. We finally had common goals.

Over the years, we learnt to pool our resources and find a balance that both of us are comfortable with. I acquired the psychological strength to quit my job and say goodbye to my salary, in return for personal growth and autonomy. He discovered the virtues of planning finances. We took loans and we returned them. We borrowed from our parents. We invested and we spent. We re-designed holidays. We kept a diary with handwritten monthly accounts and dedicated its back pages to financial goals. We revisit those goals and reset our expectations regularly. Sometimes it is all very funny all over again.

When all three of our children were in school, the administration offered a scheme where we could pay the collective fees for all their school years in advance and then receive the principal amount back when they would leave school.

He was unconvinced. I was convinced.

I withdrew a few lakhs from the savings I had made as a single, working woman and paid the fees for all three children for all the rest of their remaining school years in one go. The time had come for my husband to be impressed with my foresight and financial prowess.

'This is what I wanted to do with the money I saved when I was single and in my twenties.' Years later, I was finally able to show what I meant to the man I was in love with.

12

Learning to make money work for us

Money and love are always getting entangled with each other in our lives. Not love of money, or that money can't buy us love, but how to keep both one's money and love reserves above minimum balance in the family accounts.

It had felt like a neat closure when we used the savings of our early youth to pay our children's school fees for all their future school years in one go. We had become light and free and arrived at a place where we, the parents in the family, could afford to earn less money and therefore spend more time doing loving things together. Or just more time arguing about other things.

But let me tell you the rest of the story. Our finances were very comfortable, but we soon began to feel that our children had outgrown their school. It became imperative to intervene and offer them a more progressive environment.

This is where my extravagant husband's decision-making

skills are sharper than mine. He rarely thinks about money as a factor when he is making choices about the quality of life experiences. I trail behind because my training is to worry about money and consider it a virtue. But I watch and learn.

One by one, we withdrew all three children from the school where we didn't have to pay any monthly fees and admitted them in schools which are good, expensive, and far away from home. Now we had to pay admission fees, annual fees, quarterly fees, sports fees and buy new uniforms and books. With the money that the old school returned, we bought a new CNG car to transport the children to and from their schools everyday.

This also means that we talked a lot about money now.

Soon enough this scene played out in our home. The children have overheard us discussing how to put together their quarterly fees. We keep re-checking our emails to confirm it is really as much as we remember it is. Our tone is hushed and we are naming our various bank accounts and work projects as we discuss this.

Next, we overhear the children discuss our discussion.

'I don't know why they changed our school. They never worried about fees in the previous school.'

'This sounds like too much.'

'Maybe this time we really won't have enough to eat, like he keeps joking at other times.'

'No, I think Papa will transfer money to Mamma to pay the fees.'

'Papa doesn't have any money. He is always telling Mamma, my money is finished. Give me money.'

'That's the money in his wallet, silly. He will find some in his bank.'

At this point we stopped enjoying ourselves as an audience and dutifully reassured them that we will pay their fees without any trouble. It is okay. We are fine.

On the way, I have learnt many lessons for myself. When our children were very young we didn't want them to learn to value things in monetary terms. Things are good or bad not because of what they cost in rupees but what we receive from them in terms of experience and learning.

Now that they are on the cusp of adolescence, it is important for them to begin to know the role of money—that it has to be earned, it is limited and we learn to make choices about how to spend it. We allow them to overhear a lot of our conversations now, specially because we have also learnt how to discuss finances without being distressed.

Same lessons for the adults. Money isn't an end in itself. It isn't the most important means either. It is an enabler. Sometimes too much money disables. We stop caring to fix things that can be repaired because we can throw them away and get new ones. We don't do chores and physical work that will eventually exhilarate us, because we can pay someone else to do them for us. Soon we forget how to fix what is broken and how to do what needs to be done. We feel helpless. Aimless, too.

Without the right perspective, money becomes our favourite distraction—irrespective of whether we have enough of it or not. Thinking about it, calculating and worrying about it keeps us from paying attention to other things—those that cannot be quantified in figures, but ones that finally add up to let us know how well we lived our life in the long run.

First we work for money and then we learn to make money work for us.

I had started out being too careful about money and midway I learnt to become more careful about everything else that more often than not, money cannot buy. Like a good conversation, once in a while.

13

10 years later, the perfect anniversary gift

'Say pencil,' Naseem said to me one day.

'Pencil,' I said.

'Your shaadi is kencil,' she said, rhyming cancel with pencil.

'Oh no,' I said.

Then she went up to her father. 'Say pencil,' she said.

'No,' I yelled. 'Don't, don't. Please don't cancel his marriage,' I pleaded with Naseem.

'Why,' she said.

'Because he is married to me,' I said.

Aliza, our middle child, came to the rescue.

'Don't worry,' she said, 'you can still stay with each other.'

'Just that you won't be able to celebrate a wedding anniversary,' added Sahar, getting technical.

'Well, we can get married again,' I said.

'NO!' said Naseem. It was her turn to declare emergency.

'Don't do lippy-lippy kissie again.' Her hands waved wildly, her face contorted, she almost fell over backwards.

Afzal choked on his tea.

'If you kiss on the lips again, you will have three more children,' said Aliza.

'Six children,' said Sahar, shaking her head. 'That won't work.'

Where do these little people come from? That's all I want to know.

The older they get, the more I like to listen to them. In the 10th year of our marriage, they were 9, 7 and 4 years old.

As for us, we had learnt a few tricks too. Like balancing the lows of marriage with the highs of love. Juggling between one's gentle side and the more street-smart self.

Building a bridge from one's essential solitude towards togetherness.

'I'm not married yet, but everything you write rings true to me,' a friend texted me.

'I'm not surprised,' I wrote back to her. 'Everything we know about marriage, we found out in the first five years of our life.'

I watch our children watching us. Their attention is sharp, their insights startling. They are keen stakeholders in this venture. There are things we don't admit to ourselves that our children can spell out to us simply and articulately. And they do.

Afzal and I were discussing 'big people things' at the table. Work, money, property, cars, it must have been something like that. There was a long pause. Afzal repeated the same question a couple of times.

'I think she wants to change the topic,' said Sahar to her father.

We could have tried to dismiss her with the default adult response, 'Children don't interrupt when grown-ups are talking to each other.' But something about the sureness of her response disarmed us.

I wasn't admitting it to Afzal, he wasn't seeing it in my face, but she could see it. And she said it.

It is when we refuse to listen to children that they begin to express themselves in other ways. They get crabby, clingy and sickly. They throw tantrums and look for solace in new toys and things. We do the same as adults when we're stuck in a conflict that we are unable to fathom.

Anniversaries demand gifts and in our 10th year, I had figured I wanted an unconventional present for ourselves.

I wanted to have a few good arguments. A good fight as an act of intimacy. Fight to heal. If we cover up the cracks, they will never go away. And the cover-up always shows.

'I want to borrow some of your brash confidence,' I said to my husband. 'Some of your quick fearlessness.' Years after we exchanged vows, I wanted to exchange each other's best parts.

Also, there is some clutter I want to give away. I want to open my fists and let go of fear. Fear of hurting you, fear of being misunderstood, fear of being dismissed. Fear of being seen as fearful.

I want to let go of silences. And pretences. The ones that take up so much space, everything else crunches up into a mess in the corner.

I want to embrace...well, what should I embrace? Embrace us. That's all.

In the beginning, we love like our life depends on it. Then we learn to live, because our love depends on it.

14

Married to a Muslim—He fasts, she feasts

I'm a Hindu woman married to a Muslim man and as anyone with common sense would have predicted, our life together has its share of unexpected turns.

'It must be hard to be married to a Muslim,' friends and strangers often say rhetorically. Sometimes they lower their voice to a whisper when they speak as if they are feeling embarrassed on my behalf.

It is hard. Very hard. Specially in the month of Ramzan, when the pace of our life gets completely disrupted.

The man fasts and the woman feasts. I'll tell you about it.

Both of us set alarms on our phones to wake up in time before sehri, the pre-dawn meal that precedes a day of fasting in the month of Ramzan. I get out of bed 15 minutes earlier than him, just after 3 am. I peel a mango and pulp it. I love the whirr of the mixer in the dead of the night. I look out at the quiet, dark house from the open kitchen, enjoying the stillness. I check the time and call out to the man.

His sehri meal usually includes a glass of cold water, a mug of thick mango shake, and a cup of tea. I have mango shake too because I love mango shake even when I am half-asleep. Plus I am feeling highly empathetic.

Sometimes when I wake him up, he gestures a no with his hand on his stomach to indicate that he is still quite full after last night's meal. Now there is extra mango shake at 3.15 am. I drink my share and then drink his portion too.

Don't judge me, I'm a busy woman. Who has time to drink mango shake in the daytime?

I can already see his fasting-for-Ramzan expression when he wakes up in the morning. He walks around the home slower than usual. Reads the newspaper quietly. Then he bathes. He spreads the jahnamaz—the prayer mat—on the floor and prays. The children leave for school.

I have a cup of tea with biscuits. I try to dunk lesser biscuits than usual in my tea. I am aware of the silence as I hold my teacup. By mid-morning, I have breakfast. He is still fresh after his bath. I notice his crisp white shirt and his black reading glasses as he walks between the room that is his office and the rest of the house, organizing things for his working day.

He seems calm but I'll admit that I am quite anxious by now.

At lunch, I have the previous day's dinner and iftar leftovers. Don't be misled by the word leftovers. It is great stuff. Some of it tastes even better than last night. He is in and out of the house, visiting his various work sites. He pauses to pray.

By afternoon his legs hurt. Sometimes I read aloud to him, something I have saved up to share with him. He might fall asleep. The loud ring of his own phone wakes him up too soon. I remind myself once again to turn down the volume when he finishes his call. Sneak away his phone and put it on silent. Hide it.

By now I am also feeling the kinds of aches and pains he is describing. Maybe it is empathy, maybe it's old age. He prays again.

'Who will sit on my legs?' he asks as he lies down, looking hopefully at his children. They disperse quickly. 'My children…' he calls after them.

Sometimes I will massage his legs. 'Don't do it half-heartedly,' he will say. It is true that I am distracted. The notifications are piling up on my phone screen. Work can wait for a little, but I am tempted to respond to the friends who are pinging on WhatsApp. I wish he would really get some calm sleep. The second half of the day crawls slowly.

For the last few years, the month of Ramzan, which is determined by the lunar calendar, has been coinciding with the month of June. Believers are fasting on the longest and hottest days of the year. I follow the updates of my Muslim friends online—Sabbah in Jammu, Shubnum in Durban, Mozaffar in Chicago, Saima and Aneela in Delhi. Their self-deprecatory humour is the best part of my Ramzan.

By early evening, I start making fruit chat for iftar, the ritual that marks the breaking of the fast at sunset. Kanta, who works in our kitchen, has prepared the rest of the iftar essentials. I help myself to an advance glass of lemonade. It is refreshing, but my bones feel guilty.

'Don't be uncomfortable,' he reminds me. 'It is against the spirit of Ramzan to make anyone feel guilty.'

Some days my father will call me from his office to check on us. 'Afzal must be fasting,' he will say. 'Yes, Papa,' I will answer.

'No food? Not even water?'

'Yes, Papa, not even water.'

'Tell him to take a break, he has fasted enough now.'

'Papa, he took a break when he was travelling.'

'Tell him to take another break, this is too hard.'

'Okay, I'll tell him,' I reassure my father.

Sometimes his sister will call to check on us. 'You are not fasting, no,' she will say.

'No, I am not fasting,' I say.

'Not even one day?'

'Not even one.'

'Not even alvida jumma,' she asks, referring to the auspicious last Friday of the month of Ramzan.

'Not even alvida jumma,' I repeat after her. 'But we've got new clothes for all of us,' I reassure her.

'How are your rozas coming along,' a friend will sometimes ask casually.

'He fasts and I eats,' I often reply, smiling at my own private joke. It is ungrammatical, it breaks rules, yet it pleases me. It reminds me of falling in love with the one who fasts. There was no pressing reason to do it, it just felt good. It made us laugh.

Meanwhile, Afzal's productivity seems to peak in the last couple of hours before iftar. He is talking loudly, he visits his accountant, he makes tea for the colleagues in his office. Suddenly he snaps and now he is yelling at someone on the phone. I feel a tight knot in the pit of my stomach. I wish he would exhale. I call the children to begin to lay the table for iftar. I have a glass of water.

Finally, it is 7 pm, time for sunset. We are all seated at the dining table. The children follow the hands of the clock on the wall. They remind each other to not touch the snacks or drinks in front of them before Papa says it is okay to do so. They had briefly considered fasting with him this year. Then they decided to do a gadget-roza instead, taking a break from all internet-enabled gadgets for a week.

When it is time, he says a silent prayer and breaks his fast with dates and lemonade. There is something comforting about the slowness of this ritual. The rest of us also break our non-fast with dates and lemonade. He eats a little and goes away to pray. I get up to make tea, this time for both of us.

Half an hour later, like him, I have also eaten and drunk too much too soon. We feel bloated and heavy. We promise not to make this mistake again. Tomorrow we will eat a light iftar. We will have an early dinner like classy, mature people.

Soon he is searching for something meetha after dinner. He needs his sugar fix today, from tomorrow he will abstain. I can barely walk straight from how much I have eaten all day.

I check that there are mangoes and mango pulp for our middle-of-the-night mango shake date in a few hours. He prays for one last time before the day is over. We sleep and wake up for sehri again.

Are we different from each other? Yes. Can we still be intimate? Yes. Do we get annoyed with each other? Yes. Which one of us likes mango shake better? It is hard to tell.

III

Love Is a Growing Up

Love is a fight too. You love everyone else better when you love yourself well. You risk a fight to be able to live better.

15

Do girls make you uncomfortable?

One day, when the children were still quite little, we met a woman in an empty flat. A regular person, quite like you and me. Posh-school accent, Delhi University, an MBA and her own small business now. She was house-hunting with her husband and they were there to see a flat our friend owns in south Delhi. Our friend lives abroad, so we had gone to unlock the door for the potential new tenants.

It's a boring old chore, but when one is a family with little children, every simple outing has the potential to become a little adventure in no time.

'Hi, I am Natasha,' I said. She looked at my children. She looked at me.

'You wanted a boy,' she said to me.

I stared at her face. A question mark appeared on mine.

'You wanted a boy,' she repeated.

'No,' I said, tentatively.

I began to get the drift of what she was saying. By now she was looking directly at our youngest child, Naseem. Naseem was embracing the empty, dusty spaces in the house, humming her own song. Encircling a pillar with her hands and trying to climb it like a coconut tree, she's now treating her father like a pillar and climbing up on him. Afzal swayed for a moment like a coconut tree in a storm, then regained his balance, Naseem still hanging on to him.

'She's a girl,' said the woman. 'They are all girls.'

'Just step outside the house with me for a moment,' I said to her. I opened the main door and led the way. She didn't seem to understand.

'Come out here,' I said to her. She stepped out. 'Sahar,' I called out to our oldest daughter, 'I am just out here consoling this lady.'

'What, Mamma?' she called back from the empty cupboard she and Aliza were sitting inside.

I gestured to her. I am here, just letting you know. Play carefully. Sahar was nine and she and I read each other's faces quite well.

Now I turned to the woman who had come to see a flat but was distracted by little girls. To be accurate, distressed by little girls.

'What are you saying,' I asked her directly.

'I'm just saying that you must have wanted to have a son, that's why you tried three times,' she said.

'It may not have crossed your mind yet,' I said to her, 'but some people have children because they *want* to have children. Some people are in love with each other and become pregnant and get moony-eyed ideas about wanting to create a family together. It may be a foolish idea that doesn't always work well, but it's something that happens to a lot of us.'

'But you have three daughters,' she said. She showed me three fingers.

'Before I start feeling sorry for you,' I said to her, 'let me just cut through the crap. Do you realize how wrong it is to talk like this in front of children? You are saying to them that their parents don't want them? That they don't have a right to exist? That random strangers can be rude to them just because they are girls? What is it about them that you hate so much?'

She didn't have answers, of course. Only preconceived, borrowed ideas and conditioned responses. She's not alone. We all isolate each other, callously spitting smug, self-righteous judgements without a second thought. We have quick-stick labels for everyone, irrespective of the personal choices we may have made.

I've just figured out that one way to shut out ignorant voices is to speak louder than them. It doesn't always come naturally to me. I feel furious but my anger creeps into dark corners and hides inside me. I stumble upon it unexpectedly.

I am learning to hold on to my anger when I meet it. It is slippery and likely to get me into trouble. But really, sometimes it is better to be in trouble with others than to be troubled alone. It is critical to shake people up than be left shaking with rage oneself.

'Mamma, Papa is calling you inside.' Sahar and Aliza came out of the flat. 'What are you talking about?' Sahar asked, looking at my face for clues.

'Important things,' I said. 'Things I learnt from you.'

16

Fatherhood is a funny thing

My husband was planning a two-day trip to Amritsar and suddenly he had an idea.

'Will you come to Amritsar with me?' he asked me.

'Yes,' I said impulsively, 'let's go.' Many lifetimes ago, when we had met as two wanderers, this is how I had imagined our life together. But now I am a practical woman, so I proceeded cautiously. But what about the children? If we both get away, the children will miss too many school days.

I was assuming that our three children would have to stay with my parents while we were away and it would be too complicated for the grandparents to handle the separate school schedules.

'Let's see what days of the week these dates are,' he said, bringing the calendar from the wall to the table in front of us. The dates on which he needed to be in Amritsar turned out to be Friday and the weekend after it.

'Brilliant,' I said. 'We can leave the children with Mom and they won't miss more than one day of school.'

'This is great,' he said simultaneously, 'we can take the children along and they won't miss more than a day of school.'

'I thought you wanted to go with me,' I said, picking up a biscuit to dunk in my tea.

'Yes, but, isn't this lovely? Now we can take the children also!' Then he noticed my face.

'No,' I said.

'No?' he said.

'Yes,' I said. 'I mean no.'

He picked up a bread rusk and dunked it in his tea. 'What have you become?' he said.

I tried to explain. 'I mean, what's the point? If we go away for a short break and then spend all our energy managing the chaos of our children's hunger, toilet breaks, mood swings and interpersonal relationships, then why not do the same thing more peacefully at home only? It's cheaper.'

He looked at me like I was a lugubrious monster.

This fatherhood is a funny thing and I am going to tell you about it. In our family, it has blossomed slowly and appeared suddenly. It has surprised no one more than the father himself.

When our children were still babies, he would seem numb and slow to me. He would be there and he would look like he would rather be elsewhere. Whatever he started doing, he would take twice, thrice as long as he needed to. He would fall asleep. Deep, early sleep in which he did not hear any sounds. He was exhausted. Even discussing baby names would be a chore.

He held the babies, rocked them, burped them and shaved their little heads with his own razor. He called everyone with the good news. He helped me. I helped him.

One day he found a thought that made him feel lighter. He came to me with our firstborn infant sleeping in the crook of his elbow and said, 'When I am holding her, sometimes I feel that I am holding baby Natasha and rocking her to sleep.'

He booked tickets, he got on trains, night buses and flights. He visited friends, stayed in hotels, and started new projects without a plan.

Sometimes I fought with him and sometimes I let it be. The children waited for him. They ambushed him when he returned home. They sent him misspelt text messages from my phone. They recorded their voice messages and took their own photos on his phone for him to discover later.

'Why do I love your children so much?' he says repeatedly. He hasn't entirely understood how and when fatherhood enveloped him like a protective cloak.

'Because we are your children also, Papa.' The children never tire of his question. They always answer him.

Over the years, he has become the joy-manager of the family. He has banished hunger from our home. I make sure the basic meals are available and he is in charge of fruits, salads, sweets and savouries.

'There must always be some *whai* with our *chai*,' he announces, making '*chai ke saath whai*' a term everyone understands and relishes. He is in charge of badminton, swimming, skating, cycling and football. Also towels, combs, bedsheets, and tea sets.

'You have no idea,' he shares sometimes. 'In a traditional joint family, it is almost a taboo for a father to express love for his children. To even speak to them, touch them or be tender. It is considered selfish to be invested in your own children.'

'Papa, you are a good man,' his firstborn, who is now a teenager, says to him. 'I like you. I like you so much that I love you.'

The children were explaining a game to him in which each person had to introduce himself or herself with an adjective that started with the first letter of the person's name.

'Scintillating Sahar,' said Sahar.

'Naughty Naseem,' said Naseem.

'Agreeable Afzal,' said their father.

'Papa, you are not agreeable,' Sahar said to him.

'Of course I am,' he said.

'You are not,' she said firmly.

'I make such an effort to be agreeable,' he said, beginning to sound offended.

'Look, you are disagreeable right now,' Aliza pointed out, winning the argument hands down.

He conceded defeat and came up with another idea. 'Azaad Afzal,' he said, sounding very much like the man I know.

'You are not *azaad*,' said our youngest child. 'I own you, Papa!'

You know what I saw on the face of this once reluctant father? I saw pride. He gushed. And he agreed that he is owned by his daughters.

Sometimes, I think I could send all of them away for a short break and have a perfectly wonderful holiday all by myself at home.

17

How to create a world in which love works

For the sake of the well-being of the entire nation, I have asked my husband to be on his best behaviour for the next three months. You will be proud to hear the compelling argument I have made to back up my request.

'Please be on your best behaviour for the next three months,' I said to Afzal at the breakfast table.

He was instantly amused. 'Why?' he asked me. 'Why, why?'

'Listen, we are going to complete 15 years of being married in three months and I want to write a glorious column on the joy of relationships,' I elaborated. 'To be able to write truthfully about how stunning love can be, we have to make it wonderful first.'

'Aha!' he said, a little flabbergasted at my suggestion.

'Look, I want to speak to people who are still trying to figure out how to make this marriage thing work. I want to show them that despite its ignominious flaws, we can recover the fun and humour.'

'And I have to do all the hard work for your essay?' he asked.

'Think of the lives you can influence with your model behaviour, Afzal,' I said. 'People on the verge of despair will know that they can recover their love. You are the inspiration they need.'

Our eldest daughter cleared her throat, reminding us that she was also at the table.

'For the next three months, be like me,' Afzal said, making a quick comeback. 'Stay calm, be agreeable, don't stress and relax!'

I gulped. I didn't say what I always say–how will things get done unless somebody gets all wound up and creates pressure on the rest of the group? This is my usual justification for my angsty behaviour.

'Follow the leader,' he said. ' Eat more, eat longer, don't try to be an expert, be forgetful and dream big.'

We have a deal for now. I remind him of small details and he shows me the bigger picture. I pretend to be patient with his fantasy of living on a large farm and rearing horses one day. He pays attention when I show him the family of squirrels who have made a home on the ledge above the AC in our room. The ones who stole his socks from the balcony where they had been put out to dry.

The difference between Afzal and me is that he is the only son in an Indian family and I am the only daughter in an Indian family. He takes what he needs, knows how to allocate chores to others, receives love without having trust issues, and has the raw confidence that the world will offer him what he seeks.

Not having acquired any of these skills when I was being raised to be a good woman, I used to find him very odd in our early years. I am still sceptical, but having seen the long-term benefits of his way of being, I have agreed to copy them.

'*Shabaash,*' he sometimes says to me when he catches me at it. Even if it means I have learnt to ask him to do the work that he cannot even see needs to be done, until I have placed it right in front of him.

'Not so *shabaash,*' he feels at other times when my behaving like him makes him less comfortable.

Copying his authoritative ways makes me more relaxed and less grumpy. Copying my role of paying attention to the details has the reverse effect on him.

'I have become like you,' he complains with exasperation. 'I used to be so happy and blind. Now I can see too much. I don't know what good it does.'

I keep quiet in response.

I scoff at the patriarchal hierarchies that he is trained to honour within the family and in the world, because there is no place for women and children in that pecking order. I have first-hand experience of how systems silence women, and invisibilize the needs of children and the poor. Not being a beneficiary, I reject and rebel against it.

On the other hand, the big city hierarchies and snobberies that I am trained to participate in, exclude people like him and he is very good at calling out their injustice and hypocrisy.

Often it gets tiresome and we crave the comfort of the familiar. We long to return to the reassurance of groups, languages, jokes and etiquette that we grew up with.

This is a mountain every relationship learns to climb. Not having anticipated it, it is hard to stay even-tempered as we run out of breath and wonder if it is just simpler to return to base rather than keep trekking towards the unknown with this disagreeable person next to us.

We know that we must be equals in our relationship but our upbringing and gender conditioning hasn't quite prepared us for it. The world has raised us with different expectations. Every day it treats men and women in unequal ways. We find our needs pitted against each other's. We had thought love would mean always being on the same side. Love demands confrontation.

As the years pass, we learn to differentiate between situations that divide us and those where we are fighting to stay together. Collectively, we want to create a world that has scale, comfort, peace and justice—both for us to keep and to share. A world in which we have discovered how to make love work.

'Why do you like to remember so much?' he asks me.

'I want to reconcile,' I say. 'I want to make sense. I want to understand and accept ourselves for who we are.'

'It's 6 in the evening,' he says. 'Go out and cycle aimlessly. Come back for tea when you are relaxed. Or tired.'

He is reminding me to be less like me and more like him. For the sake of the country, I agree.

18

Write what is in your heart, Mamma

When I scold my children, and there's no point adding here that I am an enlightened parent and I don't really scold my children very often, because my children will disagree and tell you that it is not true–I do actually scold them far more than necessary, and if anyone is really enlightened in the family, it is them. This is how my sentences lose track and get derailed when I scold my children.

I detest raising my voice and scolding my children. I detest myself when I scold them. Scolding comes very naturally to me.

There are many more paragraphs already typed on this page but I am going to delete them and insert this here. I am really avoiding coming to the point today because the point is that I have a trust problem as a parent.

I have a recurring trust problem with my first-born child.

In some ways I have been treating her like she is all grown-up since she was 5. Sometimes I treat her like she is already 21. This feels great when we are sitting in a coffee shop and she is telling me about the conflicts and denouement in the life of her favourite fictional characters. It doesn't feel good at all when I find myself stalking and nagging her to make sure she isn't neglecting the details of her life outside books and movies. I repeatedly catch myself wrongly attributing motives to her. When she looks upset, my default reaction is being defensive instead of moving forward to comfort her.

'Don't behave like a teenager with me,' her father shouted at her one afternoon, as she stomped out of a conversation with him.

'I am a teenager, Papa,' she said, tearing up. 'How else am I supposed to behave?'

I am constantly surprised at how forgiving she is. I note her patience and determination to stick it out till I sort out this particular knot in my relationship with her.

One of my closest friends is a father of twin children, a boy and a girl. When his son was still an infant, he confided in me that sometimes he looks at the baby he is holding and already feels angry with him about all the bad things he will think and do as a child.

'I feel absolutely sure that he will do all the things I did secretly, and it already bothers me,' said my friend, as he tried to make sense of his irrational thoughts.

Somewhere in there is a clue. Why do mothers seem harsh and distant with their daughters? Why do fathers find themselves overreacting to their children's child-like behaviours?

We are still carrying the burden of shame and judgement that we internalized in our own growing-up years. We were judged harshly and mistrusted as adolescents and we project that mistrust on to our children subconsciously. There is a special quota of this reserved for our first-born, who find themselves on the frontline, having to endure our rantings till we wisen up or eventually mellow down.

I am exposing this trust deficit in me by writing about it here. Father Os, my teacher, would often say that it doesn't matter so much why we behave in ways that don't seem to work for us. What matters is that we stop, and we do whatever makes it stop.

Trust is a habit that we can cultivate.

In a rare moment between us, our middle child spoke to me about a family dynamic that she finds very hurtful. She is usually straightforward and blunt in her expression, but like all siblings, our children too have a secret code to protect each other steadily.

'Mamma, sometimes when we are alone, my older sister is very bossy with me. She is like a tyrant.'

'I know,' I said. 'It is a side effect of being the eldest in a group. When one has unchecked authority, it can make us very mean.'

'Yes, Mamma,' she said.

'It's hard when you are a parent also. Sometimes I am really harsh when I am alone with you children.'

'Yes, you are,' she said. 'It happens when we become class monitor also.'

'Oh God, yes! I remember when I was class monitor in

class III. I was really out of control. I used to terrorize my classmates.'

I described my authoritarian behaviour to her as a child. She told me how children in her class behave sometimes when a teacher asks them to 'mind the class' and leaves the room. We agreed that it takes maturity and wisdom to not lose it when we are powerful and others are weaker or smaller than us.

'There are ways to speak back to those in authority and reclaim our power,' I said to her. 'You are good at it.'

'Sometimes I laugh it off,' she said. 'Or I just go off on my own.'

Just now, I went up to my eldest child at her desk and told her that I was trying to write about the difficult parts of my relationship with her.

'Write what is in your heart, Mamma,' she said. 'I will read it.'

Later at night, I will sneak into her warm and enormous quilt and hold her hand as she sleeps. She and I wear the same-sized shoes now, but her hands feel small and soft in mine—just like a baby's.

19

How well do you know your mother?

My mother is no good at making herself understood. Let me rephrase that. My mother's immediate family is not very good at understanding her. All my friends seem to know her better than I do. Even those who meet her for the first time tell me insightful things about my mother.

'Now I can see where you come from,' my friend Sandhya said to me after meeting Sudha, my mother. 'I wanted to know the source,' she added. I don't always remember how strong and direct the connection between Sudha and me is. I mean, I know it, but I also forget it.

My mother was a refugee at the age of 4. She was born in Lahore and is the sixth child of her parents. My grandmother was expecting her next baby in less than a month when their family migrated from Lahore to the Indian side of Punjab in 1947. As a child, my mother spent many childhood summers living with other relatives as her parents settled and resettled in various cities, trying to create a new life from scratch and cope with the homelessness that had been thrust upon them.

Sudha is a very accessible person. She can tell her story to anyone with no hesitation. Often, her extreme comfort with strangers makes Papa and us uncomfortable, as if she were an over-friendly baby who must be protected from her own trusting self. Sudha is a survivor—she embraces situations and solves problems. She creates communities.

When we still lived in the laid-back small town in which my younger brother and I were born, Sudha would tell me many stories from her life before she was married. One story that stayed with me forever was her narration of how much her nieces and nephews had cried at the time of her *bidai*, that moment when she left her parents' home to live with my father and his family. It was a moment of great affirmation for her. She was loved and wanted by both the families that she belonged to.

As I grew up, my mother used to repeat these words to me by way of life advice: *Sabki suno, apni karo*. 'Listen to what everyone has to say, then do exactly what you want to do.'

As a teenager, I found this lame. It wasn't radical enough. I wanted to know what to do with my anger. I wanted to hear that it is okay to be angry. To retaliate and make people accountable for their words.

I had to find out how to express and sublimate my anger all by myself. For Sudha, it was radical enough to give her daughter the permission to do exactly what she wanted to do. Don't ruffle feathers, she was saying, because that will disable you from reaching where you want to go.

What has my mother become over the years? In my teenage years, when I was disturbed, confused and alienated from my mother, she seemed too far away to reach out to. In my 20s, I was guilt-ridden, having internalized that there was something that was expected from me that I was never going to be able to give. Perhaps Sudha worried similarly. In my 40s, when I present myself to my inner and outer world as a confident, articulate and sorted person, I realize that the same description fits her far better. After years of feeling misunderstood by each other, we are finally able to see ourselves reflected in the other.

If you saw how much my mother tries to compensate for those lost years when she couldn't give us more than she did, you would really judge my brothers and me. Beneficiaries of Sudha's over-efficiency, we behave like overage brats staring at our gadgets and exchanging information in some sibling code language, while she fusses over what we will eat and what our children and spouses will eat. In her 70s, she has actualized the nurturer in her. When we leave, she nurtures herself.

'Mothers are underdog people,' my friend Anubha once wrote as her status update on Facebook. Four words. I know Anubha's mother. She spends a lot of her time and energy connecting with people in distress. So does my mother. Anubha's words resonated with many others.

My mother never debates politics with anyone and she seems to have no strong opinions either. Yet, in behaviour, she is innately liberal and egalitarian. Her politics is apparent. Over the years, her choices of how she spends the money she saves and who she enables with long-term, interest-free loans that she eventually writes off is a secret best kept between her and the local tailor, *subziwala*, electrician, plumber, home-visiting beautician and her grandchildren's nanny.

The mother we have judged for being stingy is the most generous person we know. We have taken our time to recognize her empathy, to realize that she rightfully draws her sense of worth from actions and relationships that don't involve the bunch of us. Sudha is smart about money, smarter than all the rest of her family put together. She not only funds my own entrepreneurial venture, she is an angel investor for many other more deserving people.

'Who are you writing about?' our seven-year-old daughter asks me.

'My mother,' I say.

'Is she your most favourite person in the world?'

'Yes,' I say. 'But my mother doesn't know that.' My thoughts begin to get coloured by the toxic dye of historical guilt.

My daughter interrupts again.

'Who is your most-most favourite person in the whole world?'

'It is Nanoo,' I say, taking her name. I touch my head to hers. She smiles.

'And Nanoo knows that.'

Sudha and I never really hugged each other when I was younger, but I never forget to embrace her and feel her soft cheeks next to mine whenever I meet her now. I touch her a lot. It is my way of speaking to her in a way that she hears everything I say. I love you, Mom, and thank you for making me.

20

The anatomy of a lovers' tiff

One good thing about a lovers' fight is that they get so much else done. They eat less. They don't sit together for tea. They send and forward fewer messages to each other. Their work output soars. They are available for other people and places.

It's a bit of a relief after a while, because so much of the backlog clears. So many unattended chores done, things put back in their places. *Pyaar-vyaar, love-shove* is important and all, but it is quite a waste of time.

The trickiest thing about a lovers' tiff is that very soon it is hard to remember who was first hurt by whom. She cannot remember after a while whether she is offended by something he has done or whether she is the one who caused the first offence.

The fact that it is hard to believe that her glorious, sensitive self could have done anything to hurt him adds to the confusion.

Then it is time to sleep. Will he move away if she lies down next to him? Will he let her hold him when she places her hand on his body? Sometimes our bodies are smarter and calmer than our minds. They save us. She goes to sleep holding him and wakes up to find him holding her.

Is the fight over? Will they have morning tea together and move on? Is there still a residue of anger in her too? She doesn't want to drag this any more.

At breakfast, one of them brings up issues. The other answers. They are still raw. They try to go back to what started it. They are still interpreting each other wrong. Boom! They flare up again.

He raises his voice. She raises her voice. Old issues come up. Unresolved, long-term disagreements. One of them just lashes out and says horrible things about the other. One of them raises a wall and refuses to accept the accusations.

Oh man. This is not over yet.

A few hours later, it occurs to one of them that maybe this fight is necessary. Maybe it will churn things. Change something structurally. Build something better from the debris. Let the fight happen, don't throw a blanket over it.

Don't be afraid. She loves you. He loves you. Your parents are watching you from near here and from afar. The children will hold you. Fight what needs to be fought over.

Love is stronger than all this. Love needs protection. Hold on.

Another evening when they converge at home after work. Will he be ready for reconciliation? She greets him with a smile and words of love. He looks away. He has not had lunch. He won't touch the special salad she has made. He has always enjoyed it before. Dinner is tense. She feels a shiver. She goes to her room to wear another layer of clothing in the middle of dinner.

She remembers her aunt who wears warm layers and socks in summer. Epiphany. Renu aunty feels cold from rejection. The frost has reached her bones. She had managed to stay in control till her children were at home, but after they went to college and got married, the shivers reached her soul. She envelops herself all the time in the warmth of layers of clothes.

He goes out to cool off. The children are worried. The adolescent goes out to see if she can be with him. The younger child distracts herself.

She gets down on the floor in a foetal position and rocks herself. She hopes someone will find her in this corner. She has managed to calm herself down, soothe the distress of her inner child. She tries to cry, some sobs escape. She needs a tight, dark corner and a warm cover to fold herself in. She finds it. No one looks for her. This is both a relief and a disappointment.

He has slept off in the children's room while putting the child to sleep. At midnight she joins him, lying on the floor next to his mattress. He wakens and goes to his bed. She follows him there. She is determined to stay next to him, for his sake and for hers.

The morning is cold. They separate again. She takes the children with her as she leaves early for work.

He is mourning for something else he has lost. She

remains convinced of this. She cannot be angry with him. She is quiet, because he is angry with her for speaking her mind. For saying something that has triggered him.

They leave a longer gap of not speaking to each other. They talk about coordinating the children's schedule. They discuss logistics about guests they are expecting. He gives her news of the birth of a child in their family. She asks him if he has seen the email from another cousin. They pay bills online. They have put their fight in a box and are carrying it with them everywhere. They need the fight and they need to carry on.

Their children are watching them. She looks at herself from their point of view. She fixes her face. She wants them to know that it is necessary to embrace conflict regularly. To break and build again. Lose control and feel the chaos before the pieces rearrange themselves again.

Love is a fight too. You love everyone else better when you love yourself well. You risk a fight to be able to live better.

21

Who mellows first, our parents or us?

I have often drawn parallels between my father and my mother-in-law, in my attempt to understand both of them. They have both been strict and authoritarian parents, making my inner child nervous around them. They have been lavish with their love. Their daily routines have been efficient, meticulous and immersed in detail. Irrespective of their age, they have had the energy and focus to organize not only their own life, home and workspaces but also the lives of everyone else they can influence.

Ammi, my mother-in-law, died almost two years ago. On a road trip a few months ago, when we had finally left the city and were cruising along comfortably on the Yamuna Expressway, I began to miss my mother-in-law in a strange, unexpected way.

'I miss lying to Ammi,' I said to my husband, who was driving. 'By now she would have called at least twice and I would have given her reassuring, but inaccurate updates of how far we had come and when we expected to reach our destination.'

On days when Ammi knew that we were travelling, she would call and be the timekeeper of our milestones. Because I expected her to be anxious about our safety and the well-being of the children, I would sprinkle my answers with white lies. Because she always knew that I did that, she would apply her own corrections to my estimates.

'We will reach Allahabad by evening, Ammi,' I would say when we still had another uncertain 500 km to travel. 'We will watch the sun set on the confluence of the rivers.'

'I hope you reach by 10 pm at least,' she would say. 'Remember to stop for dinner or the children will fall asleep on empty stomachs.'

I picked up my phone and looked at it. As if on cue, my father's number flashed on it.

Yes!' I said, happy to get what I was pining for.

I picked up the phone and had the exact same conversation with my father. He insisted that we would be delayed. We should have woken up earlier and left home sooner. I insisted we were fine. He told me to drive carefully. I told him that we would.

'Hmm,' he said.

'I love you, Papa!' I said. He disconnected the phone in response.

I was relieved. We are still someone's children. Someone is worrying about us needlessly. Lying to our parents about small things has become the familiar security blanket that

I had begun to miss. Who would have thought that this is the detail that would bring on the pangs of loss one day.

My father surprised me recently by going against my expectations entirely. My husband, our children and I were driving on the highway on our way from our home to Jalandhar. We always get delayed, winding up our work, packing for travel and finally leaving home. Making sure that the children are fed and everyone has been to the bathroom before we leave home. I have stopped blaming ourselves for being late. This lack of guilt slows us down even more and makes us irrationally late.

On the highway in Punjab's winter, we were soon engulfed in blinding white fog. It was late evening. My brother and parents had already reached Jalandhar. My grandfather had died two days ago and the family was getting together to honour his memory.

I texted my brother instead of calling my father to update him. 'We are still near Kurukshetra,' I wrote to him, 'but don't tell Papa. We got delayed in Murthal.' My assumption was that Papa would get upset about how late we were running.

Papa replied via my brother. 'Tell them to drive very slowly. They should stop somewhere on the way and drive again tomorrow morning. Tell them to stop at Eagle Motel in Rajpura. It is a decent place.'

The man who has always said, 'Hurry up, why are you so slow, so lazy, so inefficient,' was finally asking me to take my time.

Papa has always been protective, even over-protective,

but we are used to receiving his love packaged in a stern, judgemental tone. Today Papa's protectiveness was like a gentle embrace.

Mellow Papa. Papa sending me messages from a home where his own father had just died.

Sometimes when I complain about my father to my mother, she says: 'You are no less than him. All of you are the same. Neither of you is more right than the other.'

For me, my father is many different men. He is the man who shopped for dresses, jackets, clips and hairbands for his daughter every time he travelled for work. He is the man who has judged me the most for 'doing fashion'.

Papa is always the last person in the family to endorse my decisions, and then he is the most practical and efficient about enabling me to fulfil what I have embarked upon. He is the one who didn't answer the long letters I would write to him from my early travels away from home. He is the one who will cut out every article published with my byline from the newspapers and file it away carefully.

He is both the strongest and the most fragile man in my life.

'Papa has mellowed,' I whispered to my mother when I got a moment alone with her later. 'So have you,' she whispered back.

IV
Let It Go

I'll let go of whatever it is that comes in the way of reaching out to each other when we need it the most.

22

The year of letting go

First, I called my husband. I gave him the news I had just received. Our home had been burgled. Neither of us had been at home. He had gone to his village and I was spending the weekend with my parents in Delhi. Next, I called my father.

My laptop, my data...I realize that's what I am afraid of losing the most from my home. I put a lid on the rising panic.

My next reaction is to cancel work. Postpone meetings. I want to call my editor and tell her I won't be able to submit my column on its deadline. Something stops me from doing that. Hold on to the writing. It will help you heal.

I pack our bags. Make a few more calls. Friends in our neighbourhood, friends who will deal with the police, a friend who will visit to make sure the children and I eat when we need to. He will make tea for the forensics team later and distract the children with stories. Keeping up the semblance that this violated home is still our home.

My mother arrives to meet me. She hugs me. My first tears well up. Being held by Mum is the first sign that I have permission to feel anything other than strong and calm. I am allowed to feel grief.

We drive back home with my father. Mum has handed me her iPad to take home with me. My brother helps me change my passwords.

My house has been burgled. I don't suppose they could have taken the rose plant, I think to myself. And the photographs on the wall.

'Do you still never lose your earrings,' Radhika had asked a few days ago. We have travelled together for years, video journalists with our backpacks and camera equipment. We would leave behind traces of us everywhere. Books, spectacles and lens covers. Once, even a video tape. Apparently, I never lost my earrings that I would match to my mood every day.

Well, all my earrings may be gone now. But I'm holding my daughter's hand, as she sits beside me. She turns to me. She seems stunned. I realize I am looking at myself as I look at her.

We are crossing an expressway. Papa is driving our car.

'How is this car's performance,' I ask him.

'It is good,' he says nodding. He approves. I am pleased.

2012 was the year of letting go. I weaned our youngest child. I hadn't realized how much that would depress me. I couldn't get along with anyone. Later she started school.

Mothers have a bodily reaction to separation. Just like lovers. You can keep talking to yourself to calm down, but your body speaks it own language. I was lost.

I haven't lost anything, really. I come back to the moment. Our children are with me. Everyone I love is safe. I didn't feel any fear because I was not at home when the thieves came.

I close my eyes. My search history. My favourites. My open tabs. 'Shut up,' I say to myself. No one can steal your Internet from you.

We reach home. Friends are already here. The police arrive. As I walk from room to room, I begin to take photos of the upturned mattresses, open cupboards, drawers overturned on the floor. Lists, FIR, phone calls, logistics. Send someone to get milk.

I stumble upon some things I had forgotten we still had.

The children stay outside to play in the garden. I call my husband to describe the scene to him. Drawers and cupboards are open, mattresses are askew, everything is heaped on the floor. He is relieved. We are safe. I want to be held and reassured. He makes jokes. I want to cry a little. I want him here. I can't have him here. I'm going to snap at him.

I let go of this moment. We are in different places. We have different emotional responses to the fear and relief we are feeling simultaneously. Let go.

I spend the next two days in a daze. A friend tells me I am brave. I think bravery is our default response to crisis. I want some space to be weak. I can't write unless I express that too.

I talk to friends who listen. In the middle of the night I send my husband a message. He may or may not be able to come back sooner, but I want him to know that I want him home. I'll let go of whatever it is that comes in the way of reaching out to each other when we need it the most.

I won't be afraid of being vulnerable. Ask for help. I'll take my chances and cross this creek, stepping carefully over the slippery stones. Let the cool water soak my ankles. Let go.

23

When we were too distraught to reach out to each other

They sent me home after first aid. I had a chipped front tooth and a deep gash in my inner lip where my teeth had dug into the skin. I couldn't speak the sounds that required the lips to touch each other. P, Ph, Ba, Bha.

I remember lying in bed later and discovering the magical arrangement of the consonants in the Hindi alphabet. The sounds travel from the back of the mouth towards the front. It's the fifth line that requires the lips to touch each other. I couldn't say Papa, Bhaiya, *pani* and so on. It must have been a soup and khichdi time.

Our school bus had crashed head-on into another bus on a blind turn inside Delhi's Jawaharlal Nehru University campus. The bus driver and some students in the front rows had serious injuries. My elder brother was in the back of the bus. He helped me out of my seat, picking up my bag for me. We forgot to look for my spectacles. After first aid at Safdarjung Hospital, Bhai was sent to attend class and I was sent home early in a school bus.

It was the 1980s. We did not have a phone at home. My mother opened the door around noon and saw her 12-year-old daughter standing there. Swollen face, bruised jaw, black eye. Blood on my white uniform.

'Where is Nitish?' she exclaimed. She looked behind me and down at the stairs.

'He's in class,' I mumbled. He's fine, I gestured.

She led me to bed. I didn't understand her anxiety for Bhai. This was supposed to be my moment with my mother. I was hurt.

From the moment of the impact, I must have just bided my time to the point where I would meet my mother. My Mum. And her first reaction was to look behind me. To look for Bhai.

A couple of days ago, I was reading a note from a friend describing a dream she had woken up from. I was in a bus accident once, she had written. I stopped reading.

The day of my bus accident came back to me. A doorbell rang. On one side of the door, an injured child in shock. On the other side, her unsuspecting mother.

Today, I am the same age as the mother in the scene. Like her, I have three children. I am not Natasha the child any more, as much as I am Sudha, her mother.

Sudha had sent two children safely to school. One of them returned with injuries from an accident. It took her a nanosecond to judge that Natasha is all right, she is safe.

What happened to Nitish? How badly hurt is he? Why is he not here? I want to see him. NOW.

Our older children complain to me that I never scold the youngest. 'She ruins our games, she doesn't follow any rules. She always gets to sit in your lap.'

'She's like a puppy,' I say. 'The mush in her skull hasn't developed into a human brain yet. She'll learn from you, just persevere.'

They don't look convinced. I feel angry. Guilty. I decide to set an example. I react sharply to the little one. There is yelling, stomping, whimpering. We find ourselves in the middle of a collective meltdown.

Later, I look back at the mess. Did I just lose my temper with a four-year-old for the sake of pleasing her six-year-old sibling? I sit myself down.

Sweetheart, Natasha, I think you misunderstood your role a little bit. The older children don't want you to traumatize their sister. They are saying: 'Be lovey-dovey and cootchie-cooey and weird with us the same way that you are with the little one.'

Quite the same way that I had wanted to see my mother anxious for me too, when I was hurt. When she was done being the protective tigress, I wanted her to be my gentle mother hen.

When I started writing here, I said to myself, write as if your mother is not going to read this. By now, I know I am writing a letter to my mother. And to the mother that I am.

Why do I need to revisit this story? I'm acknowledging that I felt very hurt. I'm letting go of that hurt. I'm sorry

I misunderstood Mum. I am going forth to hold her hand to make up for the times when we were too distraught to reach out to each other.

Otherwise, the little palms of my children will slip from my hands and I will not be able to tell why.

24

Children must triumph over their parents

I had never heard of the young woman in our neighbourhood till we heard the news of her death one winter morning. She had died of burn injuries in her home. Our neighbour had come over and was talking to my parents about it. Was it suicide or murder?

It was the 1980s. I was 12 years old. Almost every day there was a news story of what were termed 'dowry deaths'. The newspapers would carry a photograph of a young woman from her wedding album. Her distraught parents would accuse the in-laws of burning their daughter to death. The in-laws would claim that it had been an accident. Families that were supposed to be the secure support system for women were becoming the site of their brutal, premature deaths.

It played out similarly in our apartment complex too. As the adults around us discussed the details, we overheard that the family's immediate neighbours had been witnesses to the torture and abuse of the woman. She had been seen shivering outside her home on many nights when her in-laws would shut her out–dressed only in a petticoat and blouse and without any means to go anywhere.

Two days after her death, as my school bus slowed down to drop us back home, we saw a crowd of people outside the woman's house. Her mother was part of a women's rights group that was protesting and demanding justice.

I remember the dissonance and extreme sadness I felt. Why were her parents not alarmed enough to rescue her when she was alive? If they were crying and screaming on the street now, why did they not save their child when she was being abused? How lonely and excruciatingly painful her life and death must have been.

I was still an adolescent but the world had stopped making rational sense to me. Today I am the mother of adolescent children and it is shocking that these questions still remain relevant.

'Mamma, what is suicide?' asked our nine-year-old daughter at the lunch table last week.

'Sometimes when someone kills oneself, it is called suicide,' I said to her.

'Why do people kill themselves, Mamma?' asked her elder sister.

'Sweetheart, sometimes people feel trapped. They feel that their life will never get better. They are very sad. Or they feel that they are responsible for others in their family and they are unable to do what is expected of them.'

All three children were listening to me now. They had read the news about the suicide of Manjula Devak, a PhD scholar who hung herself in her flat at the Indian Institute of Technology, Delhi. They had seen happy photographs of her as a research scholar and wanted to know what could have been so bad that she chose death over life.

In another decade, they will themselves be young women like Devak.

'The idea that a woman represents the honour of her family is deeply flawed,' I say to my children. 'Anything that makes one feel so helpless that dying seems easier than living is wrong. It is untrue. You must reject it.

'We are wired to choose life. We don't owe anyone else their happiness.'

I'm not sure how deep to take this conversation, but I know that children hear everything that is said in the house. They are clued in to the world of adults around them in ways we don't even want to think about. Devak's parents have spoken to journalists about the demand for dowry and harassment by her in-laws.

Perhaps the greatest delusion of my life has been the belief that the world in which I was a child may have been the dark ages, but the world in which I have grown up to be an adult has to be far more enlightened and equitable than before.

Social norms and attitudes that perpetuate injustice have remained tenacious. The news remains the same. Questions that had remained unanswered when I was a child still demand answers. If I do not want my daughters to internalize that violence is the inevitable fate of women in our society, I have to find a new language to speak to them.

'Caring for myself is not self-indulgence, it is self-preservation, and that is an act of political warfare,' Audre Lorde wrote in her book of essays, *A Burst Of Light*. The first time I had read this sentence, it cut through my cultural conditioning like a sheath of light. It demolished the notion that putting everyone else's needs before one's own is a virtue to be extolled.

A family and a culture that do not enable their youth to seek their own fulfilment by giving the permission to choose who they want to be, where they want to be and with whom they want to be, is essentially asking them not to exist. Against this pressure to conform, survival is a radical action. Suicide is a rejection of the shell of a life that is unjustly being imposed on the person. It is the final act of agency of one who has had helplessness imposed upon him/her.

I turned to my children at the lunch table and spoke to them. 'One of the biggest lies of parenting is that the parents are always right. The second lie is that it is the children's responsibility to make their parents happy when they grow up.'

They listen to me in silence. A commonly repeated lament I hear from grown-ups is that ultimately all parents are defeated by their children. I want to turn this on its head. Children must triumph over their parents. It is the only way forward.

'All children must reject the narrow ideas and aspirations of their parents,' I say to my daughters. 'Be ready to be a warrior. This is how you will survive. This is how you will win.'

If I want to see change, I have to be the change myself. This is the only commitment life seeks from all of us.

25

A death in the family

The first time a child lost a parent in my class, we were in class V. I was new in that school. Priya was my best friend even though we had only known each other for a few months. I had attended her birthday party in Geetanjali Enclave in south Delhi. Her father died of kidney failure. He had had a transplant earlier.

I remember feeling numb. I didn't understand what she had lost. I was just quiet. My mother was distraught. She spoke about their family for a long time, worrying about the bereaved wife and her small children. She would repeat how young the father had been. I remembered a man with a dark beard. A 10-year-old child thinks all adults are old.

Many years later, we were film students, hanging around an inner courtyard on our campus. A classmate had had to leave suddenly after she received a phone call informing her that her mother had died in another city. I remember going into a shell again.

An argument broke out somewhere near me. Our class argued about everything. Two classmates seemed to be disagreeing vociferously over the impact of losing a parent. They were loud and angry. Hours later, we realized that both of them had lost a parent in their teenage years. They had been deeply shaken that day. You have no idea how it really feels, they were both saying. Screaming from the raw isolation of their experiences.

I had walked away that day. Both of them became my best friends later.

Our children bring home stories from their classrooms. There was a new boy in the first grade with our middle daughter. First she reported how he didn't understand English. He didn't wash his hands after going to the bathroom, the children said about him. He drank water from other children's bottles.

We spoke to our daughter. Children come from different kinds of families. They learn different kinds of behaviour at home. Some children take longer to learn the ways of a new school. Don't laugh at him. He needs friends too.

She began to tell us lighter stories. He was still being inappropriate, but they had begun to laugh with him, rather than at him. I met him after school one day and spoke to him. He looked away, his mouth slightly open. He is tall and stout but his face is still like the baby he was a few years ago.

Later, my daughter explained him to me. 'He only talks to people he knows. He listens to our class teacher, but he is shy. He will talk to me but he won't talk to you,' she said protectively.

One of our friends called us on a weekend after years of being lost to us. 'Tell him to come home,' I said to my husband. 'He needs a family. I can use a son.'

Rohit is a successful design entrepreneur. He is also a single child, a single adult and one who lost both his parents in his early 20s. He came over and stayed with us for the weekend. The first night he stayed up late, dusting and sorting everything in our house. We found toys and books arranged according to themes. 'I am always trying to build a home,' he said with a smile, in case I needed an explanation.

Life. Our stories keep converging. They intersect. They cross each other. Sometimes it takes years before we realize what it is that draws us to another. Despite our successful, sorted out external selves, something in us connects to the backstory of the other. These stories may take years to unravel, yet we subconsciously recognize something in the other.

The boy in my daughter's class. He would ask her every day how long it was before it would be lunchtime. He had difficulty in reading and writing. Girls were complaining that he irritated them.

We spoke to the class teacher about him. 'His mother died of leukaemia last month,' she told us. 'She had been in hospital for a long time.' The teacher was now making him sit next to her throughout the day. She knew he had special needs. She knew his needs.

Rohit came over one weekend and painted one of the walls on our terrace, splashing it with colours. He shot a photo feature with our children fooling around in front of it. My mother-in-law made him sit next to her and asked him about everyone in his extended family. She is a single child too.

The child in our daughter's class is changing his school. He needs a special educator, the teacher told me. Since I am a grown-up now, I don't feel numb any more. I feel that there has got to be something I can do.

'Should I do something,' I say aloud at home.

'Yes, Mamma, yes,' my children answer in chorus.

At the parent-teacher's meeting last weekend, the teacher pointed out the boy's father to me. I turned to see a young man taking his place in the classroom with a half-smile on his face. Spectacles. A pleasant, comfortable expression that made me feel relaxed and hopeful.

He had come alone. I told him that my daughter is his son's friend. We spoke about the new school his son would be going to.

'He's a wonderful child,' I said. 'We wish him luck.'

26

It's time to talk about abortion

On 28 October 2012, 31-year-old Savita Halappanavar died in a hospital in Ireland because she was denied an abortion that was critical to save her life. Halappanavar was 17 weeks pregnant when she began to experience pain and internal bleeding. Her pregnancy had become unviable, a miscarriage was inevitable and her life was at serious risk. Yet, despite repeated pleas from her family, doctors did not intervene to save her.

In 2012, abortion was illegal in Ireland, a Catholic country. Termination of pregnancy was allowed when the pregnant woman's life was at risk, but there was complete legal uncertainty about the precise circumstances in which this exception could apply. As she lay in her hospital bed, Halappanavar had begged to be saved. Despite being surrounded by the best medical facilities, she was allowed to die of ruptured membranes and septic shock to honour an outdated law that claimed to be pro-life.

Four years before Halappanavar died, I was pregnant with our third baby. In my second trimester, when I was trying to pack our bags to travel to my husband's family home in east Uttar Pradesh, I knew that I was not well.

'I have no energy,' I told my friend Shefali over the phone. 'I cannot even go to the kitchen and eat something when I feel hungry.'

'Cancel the trip,' she said, 'you can't go like this.'

'I can't,' I said. 'I have to go.'

In the bathroom, I noticed that my urine had become very dark. I didn't stop to think about it.

In the village I felt so weak, I could barely sit. In defiance, I began to walk in the courtyard. I wondered if I was just depressed and more physical activity would shake it off.

As my condition continued to deteriorate in the village, I asked my husband to arrange blood and urine test results for me. The pathologist came home with the results. 'You have jaundice,' he said, alarmed by how high my bilirubin score was.

I called my gynaecologist. She was in Jammu because her own mother was critically ill. She told me to lie down. She said, 'Just stop moving around completely and lie down in bed. Find a way to get back to Delhi as soon as possible. Get an opinion from a GP for medication for jaundice. Don't walk, don't even stand. Lie down.'

I went to our room and lay down. I sent text messages to Shefali and Manish, my younger brother. He called my mother, who spoke to my elder brother, a doctor based in San Francisco. I also had a condition called cholestatis that caused extreme itching. It felt like my body was on fire. I would draw blood on my arms and legs every day. As the bilirubin levels continued to rise in my bloodstream, I would slip in and out of deep, dark sleep and be unable to open my eyes even when I felt I was awake.

I was put on a glucose drip as I lay in bed. Our two children were five and three years old. They would come into my room and see the stand with the glucose bottle first, then me smiling feebly from behind it. They would run out quickly.

My sister-in-law sat with me all the time—talking, smiling, consoling me. Hadeesun, a friend of the family, massaged me. I fantasized about how I would help her after I had recovered. How I would remain eternally grateful to them.

One afternoon, I spoke to my husband, Afzal. I told him that if I began to sink and it became an emergency, I wanted him to save me first. 'I'm not afraid to die, but I want to live for my daughters,' I said from behind the haze of fatigue and medication. He smiled and tried to crack a weak joke.

My elder brother spoke to his colleagues and read up on high bilirubin levels in pregnancy. He raised alarms. 'Airlift her out of there,' he said. Afzal suggested that a train journey might be more relaxing. 'No, no,' Bhai said, 'in case she begins to go into coma on a night train, you will not be able to rescue her.'

At the Varanasi airport, I tried to seem as normal as possible so that our children felt safe with me. Afzal dealt with tickets, luggage and boarding passes. We went straight to my parents' home and then to hospital when we reached Delhi.

When I read about jaundice+cholestasis+pregnancy on the internet now, there are many possibilities of cause and effect that explain what was happening to me. At that time, none of my doctors was able to connect the dots for us. They told me to be prepared to terminate the pregnancy if my medical tests didn't come out right. I imagined that I would be devastated, that it would take me years to recover from the loss of this child in my womb.

After another month of being on the brink, eventually both my pregnancy and I began to stabilize. The baby began to kick around a lot in my belly. Then she was born. Small, but perfect. And very hungry. She looked around for her sisters. We named her Naseem.

When I read the news of Savita Halappanavar's plea for an emergency abortion, I followed her story with horror and rage. How could a woman's life be treated so callously despite the privilege of her circumstances? What kind of world refuses to rescue her and punishes her with death to maintain its own moral high ground?

Six years after her death, the story of Halappanavar was in the news again. In a historic referendum, 66.4% of voters opted to liberalize the highly restrictive abortion laws of Ireland that had led to Halappanavar's premature death. A video shared widely on social media showed thousands of Irish women chanting her name victoriously. 'Savita, Savita, Savita...'

'No more stigma. The veil of secrecy is lifted. No more isolation. The burden of shame is gone,' said Ireland's Prime Minister, Leo Varadkar. Like Halappanavar, Varadkar is also of Indian origin—the son of an Indian doctor and an Irish nurse.

All women know that it isn't just laws that isolate and stigmatize those who choose to seek abortions. Societies all over the world deny the legitimacy of this need. In their most vulnerable time, women find themselves abandoned, forced into secrecy and deeply dangerous situations.

Take any group of adults, give them a safe space to share their experiences, and stories of voluntary abortions done simply because the pregnancy was not at a convenient time will come tumbling out. It was too early or too late, or the gap between children wasn't enough. More than once, I have stood outside operation theatres in hospitals waiting for a friend to be wheeled out after the termination of her pregnancy. A study by *The Lancet Global Health* journal estimates that almost 80% of the estimated 15.6 million abortions in India in 2015 took place outside medical facilities, creating serious medical risks for the pregnant woman.

A pregnancy is not a woman's responsibility and burden alone. When she wants to take a decision about it, she has every right over her own body and life choices. When she needs support, the rest of her world needs to step up. It really is time for the conversation about abortion to come out in the open. No more shame. No more callousness.

27

My heart remembers what I seem to have forgotten

It took us less than a week to realize that there was no time to break the news gently to the extended family. One week, my mother told me on the phone that Rajendar, my father's youngest brother, was visiting with his sons to get some medical investigations done. On the next call, she said he had a tumour in his liver and had returned home to Jalandhar to pursue treatment. The next week, she mentioned metastatic cancer. Chachaji had very little time left.

The emotions come first. I am surprised at the waves of grief. The black hole of shock. A frantic desperation kicks in, as my cousins and we begin to search for ways to comfort him physically.

Then the lost memories begin to emerge, one story after another.

The first one is from my early adolescence–the year I turned 13. I had spent eight months that year going to the Holy Family Hospital in Delhi every day for electrical muscle stimulation and physiotherapy to revive the muscles and nerves of my right arm, which had become paralysed from a severe injury.

On most days, my father would take me to the hospital, but it always made him late for work. Some days, my mother and I would spend half a day changing public transport buses to commute to the hospital and back. During the summer break at his college, Rajendar Chachaji came to visit us from Jalandhar and volunteered to relieve both my parents by driving me to the hospital and back on my father's scooter.

Chachaji and I were an odd couple. It was hard to tell who was leading whom. He seemed fearful and lost to me as he struggled to navigate the crowded hospital systems and unfamiliar traffic of Delhi. I would guide him about alternative routes on the road and lead him from one counter at the hospital to another as we paid bills and waited in queue for my turn.

Chachaji was there to protect me and I had the same reaction towards him. Watching his determination despite his raw nervousnesss knocked me out of my own self-pity. I was distracted from my pain, and, instead of feeling helpless like a victim, I began to feel I could take charge of our situation.

As we pooled our strengths to negotiate the city every day, I felt competent. I felt loved and useful again.

In contrast to these memories from Delhi are the ones from our earlier childhood, when we would travel to Punjab to visit my father's family every year. Chachaji was the hero of those visits.

He was the youngest among the significant adults of our life when my brothers and I were children. He was the most openly loving. His presence protected us from the tense authoritativeness of our grandfather and father. He made everyone, specially the vulnerable, feel strong and important.

Rajendar Chachaji is the one who sneaked in the ice-cream breaks and took all the children to the movies and for boating. He got special passes and took my brother to watch Prakash Padukone play an exhibition match, cementing his love for the sport forever. When he discovered my love for books as a teenager, he took us to second-hand bookshops where I found Ernest Hemingway, G.B. Shaw, Somerset Maugham, Pearl S. Buck and Anne Frank for Rs 10 each. We had to buy a new bag for my fresh stash of books.

He was my mother's best friend in the home of her in-laws. Chachaji invested in joy. He was the gentlest man in our lives.

It is well past midnight and I am typing this in the home Chachaji had built with his wife and three sons in Jalandhar. My mother has been staying there for the past two weeks, supporting my bereaved aunt and her sons, my cousins. Today was the 13th day after Chachaji's death and we commemorated with public prayers and sharing of memories. Chachaji is gone and yet his presence amidst us is deeper than I have ever felt before.

In his public persona, my uncle was a professor of zoology all his life. Besides being the head of department and vice-principal of Doaba College, he also coached new batches of students for medical entrance exams every year. His students had a formidable success rate at securing admissions. As we grew up and travelled, we would meet many of his ex-students who would respond to our name by asking if we were related to Prof. R.K. Badhwar of Jalandhar.

'You are the most famous Badhwar in the family,' we would tease Chachaji. He was too humble to let that stick. Good teachers remain with us for life.

This is my fourth visit to Jalandhar with my parents and family in the last six weeks. As much as we are all grappling with a sense of loss, these trips are also infused with laughter and connections. A new generation of cousins are playing together. There is a nine-month-old baby in the house, my uncle's youngest grandchild. My mother's sisters have arrived to console her sister-in-law.

My father and I go for early morning walks together when we are here. At 75, he is still faster than me at brisk walking. He remembers routes better, makes calculations faster and stays awake longer on the 400 km-drive on the highway between Delhi and Jalandhar. 'I'm a mother,' I console myself, picking up my new nephew. 'My brain does a lot of other stuff I don't even know I do...'

Some of us go out into the neighbourhood for a break in the evening. I introduce myself as that little girl who used to visit from Kolkata when I recognize old neighbours. My aunt had taken me to her school once, proudly showing off her little niece, dressed in a child-size sari, to her colleagues.

I am surprised at how much the human heart can hold within it at the same time. How much mourning is it capable of? How many memories can it tuck away from sight, offering them back when they are relevant again?

We are drained by loss, but also somehow replenished when we mourn it. A death in the family offers us a chance to renew our relationships. With the one who has gone, with others who are still here, and also with oneself.

28

Two alone together

The days in June are long. The afternoon never seems to end. Summer vacations with our children make us think of summer vacations in our childhood years.

I must have been 14 that year. I had gone to stay with my aunt and older cousins in the far corner of the city. I had stayed away longer than the three days my father was comfortable with. He must have called my aunt's home from his office phone to call me back, because we did not have a telephone connection at home that year.

I returned home after a week of unlimited comics, long walks in the evening heat and ghost stories narrated late into the night. Papa returned from work later in the evening. His anger would have been familiar, but on that day, he looked hurt. I had never seen my father vulnerable like this.

I hung around him awkwardly and then burst into tears. He opened his arms and held me. I continued to cry with deep, heaving sobs for a while.

'You are crying as if you are getting married and going to be separated forever,' said my mother. She was uncomfortable with the high emotion.

These days, our own three children are away at my mother's home for the first time without us. Our youngest child is 5 and she is hurtling towards grown-up-ness, impatient to join the ranks of her older, more independent siblings.

'Are you sure you want to stay at Nani's without me?' I ask her. She gives me the look.

My mother informs me over the phone that the children move between video games on the desktop to those on the iPad, and then on to the TV, effortlessly throughout the day. They are busy and occupied. They have discovered the wonders of *Jhalak Dikhhla Jaa* and the IIFA film awards. Their world has expanded.

My husband and I are at home, alone and together for the first time in 10 years. We are doing just fine. We even saw a really good film together. In the opening scene, a man is shot through his head, collapsing on his desk. I distract myself by checking notifications on my phone when the drama peaks on screen. He is blinking back his tears a lot. We eat on time and sleep peacefully and get so much of our own work done. Music sounds melodious, not like another strain of cacophony in the house.

He is missing the children.

'The next time you travel on assignment, the children will stay at home just with me,' he says. I look at him.

'I'll be gone for six days only. It's a good break for the children also to be with their grandparents.'

'I'll manage on my own with them. I'll find a way. I don't like being at home without the children,' he says.

Yesterday, when he had returned home, I quickly hid behind the front door to do a loud 'Boo' as a welcome-home gesture for him. This is how our children startle him every day, pouncing on him like excited puppies. He panics and grabs me, pretending to shake with fear for a long time.

'Oh Papa, it's just me! It is what I do every day,' Naseem had said to him last time. 'You are overdoing it. Calm down now.'

I took a photo of Naseem and Sahar looking back at me from the front door on the first day that our youngest child had gone to proper school in a uniform. I put it on my blog, I shared it on Facebook and later I framed it and hung it on the living room wall. The light is so perfect, this is such a photogenic moment, I thought to myself.

A couple of days ago I glanced at this picture and my eyes smarted with tears. It is the first time the baby is leaving home. Her sister is looking out for her protectively. She turns to look at me. One day they will leave again. They will grow up.

This is the nature of love. We prepare ourselves for the day we will separate all the time that we are together.

'When you grow up, who will be my baby,' I ask Naseem, our youngest child. She is sitting on the pot in the bathroom and wants me to chat with her from a distance.

'My children will be your babies,' she says.

'I don't want your babies. I want my baby.'

'Won't you help me raise my babies?' she asks. The answer is implicit in her question.

'Okay,' I say. 'I will be a good Nani. Like your Nani.'

'And don't move from this house. My children will come and play here. Don't do like Nani, okay? She doesn't live in the house in which you were a child.'

I have no plans of staying at home when the children are gone, but I file away this request for future perusal.

29

The presence of those now absent

I have read three chapters from an English edition of the Quran this morning and then moved on to typing here. Green glass bangles tinkle on both my wrists as I angle my fingers a little awkwardly on the keyboard.

Exactly one year ago, Ammi, my mother-in-law, had passed on. I am sitting in her home, surrounded by all four of her adult children, all her grandchildren, sons-in-law, and her husband, my father-in-law.

My parents are on their way to be with us. It is early morning and most grown-ups are reading the Quran, participating in a ritual called *Quran Khwani*. It is the month of Ramzan and almost all of them are fasting. Most of the children are still asleep. The house is being cleaned and the kitchen is abuzz with preparations for the day.

In private, we are all mourning Ammi's absence. In public, we are also celebrating her presence in our lives.

On the wall next to the dining table, there are photographs from Ammi's life. She was her parents' only surviving child and is photographed next to her father in many of his formal studio portraits. In one of them, she is a nine-year-old girl, sitting between her father and uncles. It could be a black and white photo of one of my daughters. I can never walk past it without looking at the child that Ammi once was. Allahabad, 12 February 1939.

A few months after Ammi passed on, I realized for the first time that there is a purpose to death. It fills the life of those who are left behind with the words of those who are gone. It felt like a blasphemous thought. I didn't dare share it yet, but I kept it with me. I felt Ammi's presence more than ever before in my life. I had internalized the permissions I had received from her. Be beautiful, be bold, be you. You are loved. You are special.

After three months, I brought Ammi alive for me again. I began to talk about her in the present tense to new people in my life. 'My mother-in-law has sent this *chane ka halwa*,' I shared with my film crew, when actually it had been sent by her daughter from Ammi's kitchen. I brought up references to her in conversations with my children and quoted her casually. I took out the glass bangles that I used to wear only in her presence, and wore them all the time because both Ammi and I love bangles. Ammi was with me all the time now.

Wanga chada lo kudiyon, mere daata de darbar diyan, sings Arif Lohar in a Punjabi folk song popularized by its recent Coke Studio version. Bangles as a spiritual connection, as a symbol of surrender to a higher power.

As a host, I was kind to someone I didn't like because Ammi had always welcomed her. I had confronted Ammi about her a few times. 'Why do you let her behave so badly around you? She is younger than you, you should tell her off,' I had said to Ammi. She would laugh and say nothing. I realize now that this person is like Ammi's damaged child. They have a shared history that made Ammi immune to her tantrums. If Ammi had the grace to forgive, I could do it too.

Visiting Ammi's home, when she is no longer here, I realize I was also a little afraid of my mother-in-law. I must have made her nervous too. Look at us in our sociocultural context and it won't be hard to imagine why. My patriarchal upbringing has warned me since early childhood to fear the disapproval of my in-laws. I have been trained to try to please and impress the family I would marry into, and be prepared for rejection and bitterness.

This is a formula for failure, designed to perpetuate a destructive hierarchy within the family. It sets the stage for mistrust and resentment. It pits women against each other, making sure all of them lose. I reject it intellectually, but I found that I had to take it apart into little pieces and unlearn it systematically.

Ammi's love was her power. Her wisdom protected all of us.

Over the years of knowing her, I would find out more about her. I had always known Ammi only as an elderly woman, but story by story, I discovered how adventurous and young her spirit was. The woman who ostensibly lived in purdah in her marital home would travel alone with her four children every summer as a young woman. She would carrying holdalls, bedding and food for the way and change trains at odd hours to reach her parents' home. She would travel without reservation, if need be. She assumed charge and took care of her elderly parents and cousins as they battled chronic ill-health. She raised her daughter's children with the skill of practised motherhood and a grandmother's special grace.

The child in the black and white photographs on the walls of this home became a woman who inspired generations and kept the extended family together for decades.

For me, she was each of the grandmothers I had lost too soon. She went seamlessly from authoritative to nurturing in a way that adults rarely manage to do. Ammi was my bonus parent, someone whose acceptance sustained and surprised me.

'Now who will appreciate me like Ammi did,' I said to Afzal one evening, remembering how lavish her praise was for anything I did.

'I will,' he said.

'Who will love me like my Ammi?' he asked me in a quiet voice.

It's a big commitment to agree to love like Ammi. The biggest.

'I will,' I said.

Luckily for both of us, Ammi never really left our side. Her presence in our lives has become amplified by her absence.

V

Other Places

The further we travel to immerse ourselves
in an unfamiliar world, the closer
we get to our own self.

30

The long journey to find home

We were still relatively newly married when we decided to pack our bags and elope. I was seven months pregnant with our first child. We didn't know it yet, but we were on a journey to find home. To create one between us.

We arrive in Port Blair on a sunny day. The flight is turbulent and I dutifully throw up in the barf bags provided. I don't know it yet but I will be hopelessly seasick when I leave the Andaman and Nicobar islands five months later by ship. Between these two bouts of barfing though, we will discover a thousand million reasons to stay together, stay alive and stay here forever.

I live in my own cocoon in these months of pregnancy. My nesting instinct has kicked in but I have chosen to build a camper van kind of nest. In our suitcase, am carrying a woven dhurrie that I will roll on the floor of our rented home and every hotel, resort and homestay where we will unpack our bags for the next five months. I am carrying books and stationery and tank tops I expect to wear again as soon as the baby is born.

Unlike our expectations, Port Blair is a sleepy, provincial town. From our balcony, we see women with umbrellas crossing the runway at the airport in the middle of the day, taking a short cut from one part of the city to another. A fire engine visits the football field near Aberdeen Bazaar at night to water the grass. I waddle into dimly-lit, cool rooms in aquatic museums mesmerized by fish and other sea life. I can see God at work and I note in my diary that God is a designer.

We register me in the obstetrics and gynaecology OPD of the government-run GB Pant Hospital on the same day that we visit the Cellular Jail in Port Blair like tourists. The two campuses share a boundary wall. I feel intensely emotional walking past the jail cells looking at the small window in the stone wall from where inmates could see a piece of sky. We eat ice cream at the beach. He takes a photo of me. My face is still mine but my body contours are all about our soon-to-be-born daughter.

We rarely talk about the baby. He concentrates entirely on maps, routes and me. I refer to her as Baby Popo and send text messages to my brother on her behalf. He texts back to her.

Despite my preparations and all the reading I have done, the process of birthing the baby leaves me shocked. There is shock and humiliation, yelling and tears. There is nothing natural about a natural delivery, I write to my friends.

The first thing I do while I am still on the birthing table is ask to hold the baby and sing to her. She knows my voice, she knows this song. Some things do come naturally to me. On her way out, the gynaecologist tells my husband that the baby looks exactly like him.

There are no books he could have read to prepare himself. He cooks, cleans, washes clothes and goes out to send emails and make phone calls to his family. He gets his Yamaha RX 100 shipped from Delhi to Port Blair. He needs wheels. He is restless.

We go to Ross Island on the same day that we get the immunization shots for our baby at the hospital. We take a ship to Havelock Island on the day we get her birth certificate from the municipal office. I notice the inky black colour of the waters. This is where the name Kala Pani comes from.

We have stopped talking to each other in the way we are used to. Yet we have designed a formula that makes us stick to each other. We may have lost the words between us but we still have to figure out the routes we take every day. Make decisions about meals. Get photos printed and mail them to Ammi, his mother. We are distracted by external challenges.

At some point, we calm down and begin to recognize each other again. After the helplessness and desperation of the first few weeks, I have learnt to demand-feed the baby anytime, anywhere. He has learnt to burp her and rock her to sleep. We are world champions at changing diapers by the roadside.

Before the rain reaches us, I see tranches of it sweeping towards us from a distance. On our bike we drive to national parks and reach places from where he can go for short treks. He wants to go snorkelling but the idea makes me panic. Baby sleeps in a hammock, swaddled in my soft blue Bandhini dupatta. I take photos of her beatific face. He returns from snorkelling and tells me that he didn't enjoy himself like he expected to.

Sometimes it feels lonely, and sometimes the silence is extraordinarily comforting. There is always baby. Gentle, smiling baby, responding to my gibberish, being comforted by his touch. Teaching us to stay in control. Stay together.

We have discovered a dhaba where we eat a dosa and fried fish thali for Rs 20 every day. I am still eating more than him and it makes me very happy. The tank tops can wait.

We travel to Little Andaman sitting on the floor of a ship for 9 hours with hundreds of island people. We hear Bangla, Tamil, Kannada and the distinct east UP accented Hindi around us. On the island, we go to meet the original inhabitants of Little Andaman. An Onge woman holds my baby and I hold hers. We have no other language to speak to each other. Their poverty is heartbreaking.

We sit on the rocks by the beach looking out at the dance of the waves. I soak in shades of purple, lilac, aqua and green. They cleanse the clutter in my head. This light and these colours will always stay with me.

There is a lesson in being face to face with the drastic beauty of nature that isn't always translatable into words. The silence it inspires is a conversation with the self.

Home is a place you create inside yourself, we discover. It is a landing ground whenever we need to touch base with our own selves. The further we travel to immerse ourselves in an unfamiliar world, the closer we get to ourselves.

31

Take the slow train home

'But I don't want you to die in pieces, Papa,' exclaims our five-year-old child. This is why I don't miss watching TV dramas any more.

We are packing to catch a train to Mumbai. A friend is getting married and we decide we must bestow our blessings in person. There is wet laundry to be brought in and laid out over the furniture before we leave. Unironed saris, dupattas, golden sandals and hairbands are tucked into suitcases. Food, toiletries, books and phone chargers go into backpacks. Our first-born child is alert and tense, doing her own thing as well as running errands for me. The youngest is recovering from viral fever and screams in horror every time she wipes her nose. Her skin is raw from excessive wiping. My voice is getting edgier as we get closer to the deadline to leave home.

Our middle child starts bawling. 'I don't want to go to

Bombay,' she wails. '*Mujhe kaheen nahi jaana* (I don't want to go anywhere)!'

Her father holds her. She is hungry. Tired from a long day in school and lost in the chaos at home.

We will spend tonight sleeping on the train. We have four berths reserved on the train and we are five.

'Children,' says their father, 'will one of you share the berth with Mamma or me on the train?'

'Papa! Papa! Papa!' come three voices from different corners of the house.

'Natasha, did you hear that? Now I can die in peace,' says my husband.

'But I don't want you to die in pieces, Papa,' says the youngest. It takes a while for the laughter to die down.

What have you been doing recently, a friend will ask, and often I find myself unable to form a coherent sentence as a reply. Life seems like a whirl, every choice imperative and overlapping with many others. We are always hurrying and rushing the children yet we find ourselves stressing in traffic, always late for everything.

This trip to Mumbai is our attempt to cheat the whirl. We have booked ourselves on the slowest trains we could find. We will spend two days and two nights just being on trains in the company of each other.

The next morning, I wake up to see our youngest child looking out of the train window, her chin and arms resting comfortably on her sleeping father.

'I saw sheep,' she says. I take a photo of her.

Her older sister says good morning from the upper berth. In reply, I take another photo. The light is glorious.

Gentle brown hills outside the window. Then bare flatlands. The rural landscape is neat. We know we are approaching a town when we see garbage piles near the tracks. Mustard fields glow fluorescent yellow-green in the morning light. I might see a different shade if I take out my glasses and wear them, but I'll have to take them off to look into my camera, so I let it be. The rumble of the train's wheels on the tracks. Every now and then a jerk in the rhythm.

'*Chai, chai, chai*,' says the chaiwalla.

'*Do chai*,' I say. Two teas.

The children mimic the chaiwalla's chants. I join them.

'Make your mouth *dheela*,' Naseem tells me. 'Leave it loose and say *chai chai chai*.' I follow her instructions.

'*Naashta, naashta*,' says the man selling breakfast in a nasal voice. We get upma, bread-omelette and extra sauce. At Vadodara station we buy dhokla, pakode, ice cream, spiced buttermilk and chocolate. I stand near my coach, in a sliver of sun on the platform, warming my feet. I buy guavas.

Our appetites are insatiable. We have forgotten the wedding card at home. The bride-to-be sends us her address and instructions by text.

'What is this station?' I ask, admiring a wide, neat platform with steel benches.

We are in Godhra. My husband and I look at each other. I remember where I was standing when I read the headlines about the fire in a train coach on Godhra railway station in 2002 setting off a backlash against Muslims that left over a thousand people dead in the Gujarat pogrom.

Fifty nine Hindu pilgrims had died, setting off a backlash that resulted in the Gujarat riots. I pick up my phone, a default response to stress. Coincidentally, it is 6 December, 2013. Two decades since the Babri Masjid was demolished by Hindu arsonists leading to riots in several parts of the country.

I read a friend's Facebook update. 'I don't want to look back,' she has written.

'Mamma what should I make?' says Naseem, adjusting her drawing book in her lap. Her elder sisters are reading J.K. Rowling's Harry Potter series again.

'Make a bridge,' I say. She colours a river in spate. Fish in the water, birds in the sky, the sun and a bridge.

We cross the Narmada near Bharuch. It is so wide. I cannot stop talking about it. Boatmen in boats are resting in the shade under the bridge. We see a mosque, a gurdwara and a temple on its banks. Egrets on trees.

The children count the boats and cannot agree on a final number. They are getting restless now.

'Lower your voice, people are resting,' I say to them once again. I tell myself to stop telling them to lower their voice.

'Next time we will get Uno.' They play some complicated game they have learnt in school.

I go to sleep against the odds. I wake up to see scarecrows on duty in their stiff white *kurtas*. Orchards. Buffaloes and their new calves. Two of our children are sitting on their father's legs. He is asleep.

This train journey is an oasis in our life. We are in no hurry to get anywhere. We are on our way and we are at rest. We are at home when we are together.

32

Mountains, meadows and memories

We met a shepherd in Bedni, a Himalayan Alpine meadow at 11,000 ft in Chamoli district. I was fascinated by how similar my husband and he looked as they stood chatting on a gentle mountain slope, their profiles silhouetted against the evening sky. We were more than 500 km away from our home and the shepherd was in his home. We were jubilant and exhausted, we had just reached the highest point in our trek. For the shepherd, it was the end of yet another summer day. It was time to herd his sheep back into their pen.

There were snow-capped mountains in the far distance and sheep on the slope I was on. The light of the setting sun formed a golden rim on their woolly silhouettes. The grass below their hooves was aglow. Instead of sinking calmly, the sun had set the horizon on fire.

As my attention returned to the conversation, we

discovered that the shepherd had lived in our neighbourhood for three years.

'After school, I tried to get into the army, but I didn't qualify in the entrance exams,' he said. 'My father had been in the army. I went to Delhi to find work and lived in Greater Noida for three years. I worked for Moser Baer, LG and Honda. The money was decent but I saved nothing. I shared a room with other migrants like me.'

I imagined the room in one of the densely populated villages that have been surrounded by the acquisition and development of agricultural land around them. Our driver, Idris, lived in one of them and preferred to spend all his time in parks after work hours.

'I came back for the *thandi hawa*,' said the shepherd. 'The cool breeze.'

My husband discussed the arithmetic of his sheep rearing business with him. He said he saved about Rs 2-3 lakh a year. His living expenses in the mountains were minimal. If and when he decided to return closer to a city for his children's education in a few years, he would have good money to invest in a livelihood there.

'How do you keep track of your sheep?' I asked him.

'I recognize them by face,' he said. 'If one schoolchild goes missing, everyone will know which child is missing. Like that, I know my sheep. It is impossible to count them. I cannot make them stand in a queue.'

His analogy made perfect sense at the time. I typed notes into my phone later that night, but I forgot to write down his name.

A year later, as I revisit memories of the trek, it is amusing to see what remains with us after so much else is lost through memory's sieve.

Mules and dogs, butterflies and eagles had been comforting companions. Our trekking guides' dogs particularly, who would race ahead and then come back to the group, meeting each member as if they were taking a headcount.

The tinkling of bells around the neck of the grazing animals. The smell of food and the sputter of fire. The security of potatoes and rice. A lake on the first day and a river at the end.

I remember the cold of the water when I first put my hand into a mountain stream. My legs were like lead, my back wasn't speaking to me any more, but my hand in the stream was alive. I took a photo of it. My thin hand, a blue ring, the waves of light in the cold water. I can walk through forests and scale mountains again for that sensation.

I remember that my husband and I had private arguments over tea. After the tents had been set up and everyone had a place to rest, I was cranky that even though we had tea twice a day, the tea was no good. I'm not sure what he was angry about but he had no tolerance for my whining. I, on the other hand, felt so accomplished at the end of every day of scaling heights with my parents, my children, my niece and my sisters-in-law, that I felt it was almost cute that the tea was making me break down. I was ready to empathize with the man who was on a trek with his parents-in-law, but he would not give me any leeway to complain about the tea.

Maybe it was altitude sickness. It was a mystery. One of those couple moments when you are doing so well overall and yet you can ruin the present by fighting over the quality of tea. Does it make sense?

I don't know about sense, but it does happen a lot, I can hear you answer as you read this.

On our way down, we stopped at a two-storeyed home in a village where there was a grocery shop in one room. Our children watched me buy almost everything the shop stocked—biscuits, chips, packaged juices and other assorted edible things.

'When we travel, you always buy us things you don't allow at home,' my daughter said to me.

'That's true,' I said, proud of myself. We both thought about what she had said. I didn't have any words to explain myself.

'I found out what all I am still capable of,' my father said, sitting down to rest. 'I had written myself off. But no, I have a lot left in me.' At 70, he had triumphed over his varicose veins.

My mother was chatting with an elderly woman who was sitting outside the home. The woman must have asked her where she was from. My usually reticent mum was telling her the story of her life, starting from a village near Lahore to every town and city she had lived in, first as part of a refugee family in north India and later as the wife of my father, an engineer in the steel industry.

A younger me would have been embarrassed. Now I listened to her looking back at her life from the distance of the mountains. Sharing her story with someone she had just met. Just like the shepherd, travelling away from home had brought her closer to all the places where she truly belonged.

33

Rajma, potatoes and a fistful of fears

In the middle of our holiday in the mountains, we stopped at a brook gurgling down between two slopes along the road to Barot in Himachal Pradesh. Like a magnet seeking its opposite pole, I walked up closer to the source of the stream. As the water gushed over a rocky bed, its surface had become wavy and undulating. Dappled sunlight created the familiar pattern of scales on a reptile's skin.

I put my hand under the surface to let the light and water glide on my palm. As if I was allowing a snake to pass over my hand in peace. As if I was letting go of something I had held too tightly. A fistful of fears, perhaps.

Is it still a holiday if you take your worries and entanglements with you? At the stage of life we are at, it is a real holiday for us when we can be alone with just ourselves as a family—no doorbell, no deadlines, no phone calls to return. No other commitments.

This time our family baggage included one child's allergies, another's anxiety, everyone's exhaustion, and a collective desire to fly and be free. Even if that meant long days of driving on highways and listening to the same playlists. So long as it included lots of experiments with food, deep sleep and spurts of good conversation.

It was Diwali break in schools and instead of driving straight to our friends' home in the mountains, we stopped for the night in Anandpur Sahib.

I was very enthusiastic about visiting the Virasat-e-Khalsa, the awe-inspiring museum of Sikhism in town, but as soon as morning dawned, I realized that all I wanted to do was go to the Anandpur Sahib gurdwara with my family. I remembered my mother's enthusiasm about visiting gurdwaras everywhere we travelled as children, and tried to look less excited than I was feeling.

As the children lined up to let their father cover their heads by tying borrowed scarves around their chins, I took photographs of the moment. We relaxed and listened to gurbani together, creating new memories for another generation in the family.

As we left Punjab behind and drove into the Kangra valley, I tried to convince our children once again of the charm of travelling in state transport buses.

'One day we will do road trips by bus,' I said.

They reacted as if I was suggesting a stint in a gas chamber.

'*Arre*, you don't know anything yet,' I said, trying to articulate the charm of listening to local music on dusty, bumpy, unpredictable bus trips through India's countryside. I wondered at my own self. What makes our memories acquire the soft sepia tone of nostalgia? What are we trying to recreate when we attempt to relive our own childhood with our children?

The next day, our hosts suggested paragliding from Bir Billing, and everyone was immediately enthusiastic. Except me. Secretly, I laughed at myself again. I wanted to stay on the ground as my husband and children flew off cliffs with professional pilots behind them, as if my staying on the ground and staring at them was going to keep them safe. I distracted myself with a Maggi treat in Billing as my family soared in the skies above.

Sometimes you know your holiday is going well even though you may be acting like a grump. You take all of yourself on a holiday—the part desperate to relax, the one ready for adventure and the one that is knotted up and heavy with unresolved grief. I ordered a honey-lemon-ginger tea to detox after the instant noodles.

Our children watched our hosts set up a telescope and together they gazed at the stars as I slept inside, soft and cosy in my bed. With their new friends, the children learnt to identify constellations. They saw the Milky Way and wondered how we can see something far in the sky if the earth is itself a part of it.

The next evening, everyone took turns to admire Saturn and its rings through the telescope. When I squinted into the viewfinder, all I could see was a small, blurred paper clip in the evening sky. Is this what everyone else was so excited about?

We bought potatoes from a field from a woman farmer who was harvesting and packing them in sacks to send to the market. I became besotted with rajma (kidney beans) in Barot and its upper villages. We stopped our car to admire the rajma plants growing in the fields. Different-coloured beans were drying in the sun in the courtyards of village homes. We had a divine rajma-chawal lunch at an eatery, 5,000ft above sea level.

'Why are you wearing my sweatshirt?' asked my husband, as we were changing into our nightclothes after a long day in the Barot valley.

'I've been wearing this every winter for two years now,' I said. 'It is practically mine.'

'*Yeh toh beimani hai*,' he said. 'This is not fair.'

'It is all perfectly square and fair,' I mumbled, as we snuggled into bed.

34

Speaking Hindi in China—Languages that flow in our veins

Travelling in China for the first time, I spoke to everyone in Hindi. After a stressful first day of deliberately speaking broken English and trying to mask my Indian accent to make myself understood, I realized that speaking calmly in Hindi led to better communication and kept me humane.

In the shops, hotels and streets of Shanghai, where English was not the bridge I had expected, I chatted with everyone in Hindi. My brother was using translation apps on his smartphone which were quite efficient, but I would often beat him in getting the point across.

'*Do mango shake de dijiye* (two mango shakes please),' I said to the man at the fresh juice corner shop in Shanghai, pointing to the correct photo in his menu card. He made us delicious, fresh mango shakes. '*Langda aam*,' I said to him, and he agreed with a wide smile.

'*Yeh khiloney Lajpat Nagar mein bhi milte hain* (These toys are available in Lajpat Nagar as well),' I shook my head and said to the man offering to sell plastic Minions with a helicopter fan attached to their head. In response, he offered to sell me the toys at Lajpat Nagar prices. He won.

'*Bhaisahab, hum aapko bewakoof lagte hain kya, aap kaisi baat kartein hain* (Brother, do we look like fools to you, what are you saying)?' I said to the conman offering to sell us sealed boxes of iPhone 6s at Shanghai airport when we were leaving. He laughed nervously, perhaps even fearfully.

This was a high point in my relationship with Hindustani, a language I want to own but have lost somewhere in the labyrinth of my growing-up years. We got along fabulously in China.

The first language I was born to is Punjabi. My parents and grandparents speak to each other in Punjabi. My second language is Hindi. Adults in our family spoke to my brothers and me in Hindi.

My third language is English, which I learnt in school. I discovered the world and myself in English. It is the only language I can write fluently in. English behaved like a colonizer. To use a familiar analogy, English gave me a railway network that took me far and deep, but it also usurped the Hindi and Punjabi spaces in my expression, leaving me with only one language that seemed to work properly.

My fourth language is Urdu. My mother-in-law used to speak to me in Urdu. She blessed my children and me in Urdu, enveloping us protectively in her world. When Ammi and her son spoke to each other in Urdu, sometimes I only understood the prepositions. And yet, Urdu poetry reaches places that are inaccessible to other languages. It touches unacknowledged grief and nameless pain. The voices of Nayyara Noor and Rekha Bhardwaj, of Ghulam Ali and Ali Noor, flow like river water breaching through the crevices of dams.

'*Dil dhadakne ka sabab yaad aaya, woh teri yaad thi, ab yaad aaya...* (I suddenly remembered the reason why my heart was beating like that. It was your memory, I suddenly remembered that).'

When we lose a language, it's like forgetting a route in a forest that used to be familiar to us. We want to explore parts we used to know, but we can't seem to find the access. Distant memories and echoes of laughter beckon us. There is a dull ache for something intangible that we seek to recover.

Punjabi came back to me in the voice of Nusrat Fateh Ali Khan. Punjabi is my most broken language, yet it is also the one that yields the most laughs in my adult life. I was travelling in Kashmir, nursing a broken heart, when the voice of Nusrat Fateh Ali Khan singing a qawwali in Punjabi on my headphones stirred my attention. I had just received a new collection of cassettes from Karachi. As my taxi drove around mountain bends, Urdu and Punjabi words intertwined together in poetry that healed. The pieces of my disjointed, broken worlds came together in the rising crescendo of a Punjabi qawwali.

One of my closest friendships in adulthood pivots on our shared Punjabi childhoods. Rohit and I speak amateur

Punjabi with each other, often recalling the imaginative taunts of angry aunts and alcoholic uncles and collapsing with laughter. The humour is part bitter and largely liberating.

Of all the languages I have lost, I miss Hindi the most. I married a man who speaks Hindustani, so that my children would have Hindi running through their veins. For the first few years of their life, I spoke to our children exclusively in Hindi. Then I needed to scold them, and true to its form, English proved to be the most useful language when I needed to raise my voice.

My friend Aneela, who grew up in Rawalpindi in Pakistan and lives in Delhi, travels all over the world speaking to her Australian-born son in Pushto. He talks to her in English.

'I speak to Arhaan in Pushto because I didn't know any other way when I first became a mother. I never insist that he reply in Pushto. Thank God he is talking to me, has been my main response to whatever he says,' jokes Aneela.

I wonder if Arhaan will always have two language compartments in his soul. One for the warm Pushto his mother speaks to him in, and the other for the vocabulary of the rest of the world.

Aneela confides that she even speaks to cats and dogs in Pushto. I know my Bengali friends speak to their pets in Bangla. I cannot imagine talking to my adopted street dogs in Punjabi, a language more familiar to my ears than to my tongue.

My Hindustani has recovered enough to become the language of my emotional expression. I use its vocabulary to express hospitality and show respect. The swear words in my head are all in Hindi. I feel at home in Hindi. Authentic. Therefore, I travelled in China in Hindi. When there was no other language to connect us, it was best to use the one my emotions are most fluent in.

Speaking to Chinese people in Hindi, I felt completely free. I was a better person, smiling and being affable with everyone. I was more talkative than usual, commenting on wonderful food and telling people my personal woes. Nobody recognized my words, but I swear I felt understood.

There are languages that we know how to speak. There are languages that know how to speak us. Languages that we understand, and those that understand us. Recovering lost words makes us whole, bringing alive parts that had lost their voice.

Now you tell me the story of languages that flow in your veins.

35

Pakistan—What's there not to love?

Pakistanis love Boroline. Do you remember Boroline? It is a soft, white cream that comes in a dark green tube with a flower-shaped round black lid. It smells of childhood.

They love Himalaya toiletries, Khadi handmade soaps, Pudin Hara and Hajmola. Suits in pastel shades with Chikan embroidery are highly coveted and you will not believe how devoted Pakistani women are to imitation Kundan jewellery from pigeonhole shops in the old cities of Lucknow and Delhi. For their men, they like dark Fabindia kurtas in size XXL.

If you are a Pakistani and this list makes no sense to you, then you are probably not my Pakistani relative. Most of them are based in Karachi and are originally from Uttar Pradesh or Bihar. They are charming and fun. They love Indian street food but never confuse chhole-bhature or sambhar-dosa with a real meal. Snacking is for entertainment, fruits are for decoration, but real nutrition only comes from proper meals. They love paan and participate in searching for good paan everywhere they travel in India. It is safe to say that they are into food. This is also why they have grudging respect for supplements like Hing Goli and Isabgol.

When you visit them, do not offend them by not eating enough. I have done it once by having only dal-chawal at a feast hosted in my honour and now I am afraid to visit them again. They are very generous with gifts. Sometimes the *khussas* (handmade leather slip-ons with embroidered or painted uppers) are the wrong size but they are so beautiful that you keep them forever.

Their children love binge-watching American drama series and uploading hashtagged photos on Instagram. They carry their own packets of chips and Oreo and consume all the Wi-Fi in your home. Some of them wear more foundation than their peerless skin requires. They love shopping and I have no clue how they deal with storage in their homes or remember where their things are. They have the first position in the world as far as the size of their suitcases is concerned.

I also know many Pakistanis who are not my relatives. Posh Pakistanis are very posh. Really, there is no Indian who has not spent his or her first visit to Pakistan just gawking at how worldly-wise, good-looking, fashionable, literary, articulate, comfortable and friendly Pakistanis seem to be. They also laugh full-throated laughs, leaving us wondering where to hide the pieces of our shattered notion of India's superiority over neighbours. They make us feel not-posh-enough.

Besides the elite, urban upper class, I know another Pakistan. In 2007, I conducted a workshop in documentary film-making at the Interactive Resource Centre (IRC) in Lahore. When Farjad Nabi, a film-maker who was consulting for IRC, first called to invite me, I told him that the only thing I wanted in return was four visas for my family. Armed with an invitation letter from IRC's Mohammad Waseem, I went to the high commission of Pakistan in Delhi and behaved very agreeably. I endorsed the Deputy High Commissioner's opinion that everything was better in Pakistan, particularly the prices of vegetables in his hometown, Jhang, versus those in Delhi's Khan Market. He gave us non-reporting visas to Lahore.

In my class at IRC, there were trainees from rural areas near Mardan, Multan, Peshawar, Larkana, Gujranwala, Hyderabad and many other far-flung cities of Pakistan. There were young men and women. There were Muslims, Christians and Hindus. They reminded me of trainees I had worked with in Bhilai in Chhattisgarh. The same energy and insights and an organic aptitude for their cameras and editing software. The same combination that every workshop has of the very quiet techie, the theatrical performer, the friendly asker of too many questions, the slow and steady one, and the enthusiastic trainee who gives a demonstration of all the mistakes one can make.

Madiha and Nazish were two women from Mardan in the Khyber Pakhtunkhwa province. Madiha arrived in class well-dressed, with her waist-long hair open and wearing high heels. Within a few hours, I was sending off all the trainees in groups to take their first set of shots on the streets outside. As I handed a video camera and tripod to Madiha's team, I asked her to change into comfortable footwear.

'Oh I'm okay,' she said.

'Do you want to tie your hair?' I said.

'No,' she said. She smiled confidently and walked away.

I judged Madiha. I had no doubt that women can be excellent video journalists, but I did expect them to dress for the role. I had done it myself, always wearing running shoes and loose practical clothes when I went on location as a cameraperson.

Madiha turned out to be a natural. She conducted interviews effortlessly and had a natural talent for composition and shots. I looked at her work and came face to face with my own biases against women. Despite being a professional who had broken gender barriers to become a news videographer in India, I had internalized that my femininity would come in the way of my ability to be proficient at work. I could be identified by my baseball cap and sports shoes whenever I was on location. Madiha taught me a life lesson.

Later, when we became friends and I confessed my bias to her, Madiha told me that she had indeed changed her entire dress code to work in Lahore. She worked as a radio presenter in Mardan and every time she had to step out for an interview, she would cover herself from top to toe in an abaya and a veil.

'In Lahore, no one would take me seriously if I stepped out like that,' she said. Her long open hair, her colourful clothes and stilettos were liberating for her. Later, Nazish and Madiha made a film called *Two Women And A Camera* to document the growing restrictions in the lives of the Pashtun women of Khyber Pakhtunkhwa. It was edited in Delhi by the acclaimed film-maker Reena Mohan. I learnt from Madiha that you don't have to peel off your skin and become someone else to do good work. You can be you. It works.

From the same workshop, Sadar Jan, who is from a town in Sindh called Dadu, continues to send me links of the documentaries they have made over the years. I show them to students and trainees in India. A mother battles poverty and drug abuse in a slum in Karachi. Another woman dresses up as a man every day to cycle to work. An orphan in a village makes a living singing the songs of Kumar Sanu from Bollywood films. A transgender person laughs, cries and dances as she shares a day in her life. Dying crafts are documented along with the stoic pride of their craftspersons. Our stories in India aren't that different from those in Pakistan.

In Lahore for the first time, my husband was fascinated by the Punjabis. He was in awe of the combination of the Punjabi language with Lahore's extreme etiquette, humility and literary fluency. Pakistan's Punjabis broke every silly stereotype he had harboured, having only been exposed to the variety called 'Delhi Punjabis' till then.

What else do I know about Pakistan? Pakistanis are very witty and get extra points for being very good at laughing at their own selves. They love cats and their country. You don't need me to mention *Coke Studio*. *Coke Studio* music and their videos are like a modern shrine where the ancient spirits of our shared culture are channelled. *Coke Studio* touches even those who don't understand a single word of the lyrics.

On assignment for work in Almaty in Kazakhstan, I became friends with Nasim Zehra, a journalist from Pakistan. Later, we met again in Delhi and Lahore. She brought me silver earrings from Lebanon. I told her that we had named our youngest child Naseem.

When Indians and Pakistanis meet outside their own countries, they discover that they have a natural affinity for each other. It's the same when we find each other on social media. We get each other's jokes. We get each other, even though we have heard many times that we aren't supposed to.

Hate doesn't come easily to everyone. It isn't a failing on our parts, you know, it's a privilege we have. Just hold on to it.

VI
Other Loves

All this leftover love one feels, you want to give it away before it is too late. There is only one life and the survivor can never forget that again.

36

Roger Ebert and me—How tragedy and Twitter bonded strangers

Some stories seem so implausible that even as they unfold around us in real life, we refuse to believe them. Our doubt makes us hesitant to share them. We love grand stories in the movies, but we hold on to our cynicism in real life. It is safer, perhaps. It is also cowardly.

I didn't grow up watching Roger Ebert on television. Unlike many others in India, I had never read him either.

Then one day, after about 8 months of having created a Twitter account, I followed him on Twitter. It was the year 2010. The Oscar Awards had just been announced and I had seen many of his tweets re-tweeted to my timeline.

The act of following @ebertchicago, the hugely popular American film critic, changed my life forever. Twitter had been my secret writing place for a few months. I was writing there without always understanding what the words conveyed. There were feelings, anecdotes, conflicts, moments. I had 60 followers and most of them were not active. I knew no one there. I hadn't bothered to find out how Twitter worked. I had never checked my mentions column or any other notifications.

The brevity of the medium was a literary challenge I had set for myself. Say it in exactly 140 characters.

I checked my email a few hours later. I thought it was Twitter's birthday or something. I had a few hundred new followers. What's going on here, I thought. Who are these people? I scrolled down and right at the bottom was the first email, which said: Roger Ebert is following you.

I picked up the phone to call my brother. I put it down. I looked at that mail again. I looked at Twitter. Roger Ebert had read me before I had had a chance to read Roger Ebert. He had scrolled down my Twitter timeline, something about my tweets had resonated with him and he had RT-ed some of them. It was the beginning of a very precious connection that is making my eyes well up with tears right now.

Over the next year, Roger Ebert kept on retweeting my tweets, new follower mails kept falling into my mailbox, I became hooked to *mentions* and I wondered how long this was going to last. Roger Ebert seemed to understand my words in a manner that I certainly didn't.

In 2010, Ebert was newly recovering from cancer and surgeries that had removed his lower jaw, taking away his ability to speak and eat. He was embracing life anew, reconnecting with the world via the Internet with an urgency and generosity of spirit that so many people would witness firsthand.

Reading and writing became Roger Ebert's superpowers. His legendary ability to see the whole film in its first shot was now turned towards the people he met on the Internet.

Loss that leaves behind depression and melancholy also offers us the great gift of perception. An instant ability to spot the truth. Honesty. Love. You have been this close to losing it all. Your fears and pretensions have been peeled off you. Your mask has fallen off.

I knew because I was in similar emotional terrain. Roger Ebert looked at my words and he saw that in one go. As one recovers from trauma, one returns with a sharp sensitivity towards every moment of beauty. Every turn of phrase, the dance of light on the leaves, the flicker in the lizard's eye before it darts away.

Roger Ebert was writing, blogging, tweeting to make himself whole again. So was I. We were both in a kind of personal rehab and there was an instant connection. He searched online and tweeted the only films I had uploaded at that time. I had a secret blog that had been seen by two people besides me. He asked me to show it to him. 'There is a great novel in this blog,' he wrote.

Twitter featured my account on its homepage. 'You are a great teacher,' I wrote to thank him. He replied: 'I am a better student.' I said: 'You inspire me.' He answered: ' I'm a good reader .'

He blogged about how Twitter had become a substitute for the real-life conversation he missed. 'When you think about it,' he wrote, 'Twitter is something like a casual conversation among friends over dinner: Jokes, gossip, idle chatter, despair, philosophy, snark, outrage, news bulletins, mourning the dead, passing the time, remembering favourite lines, revealing yourself.'

He celebrated the connections he had made online and mentioned me too. I wrote back to him, revealing a story I had not articulated even to myself.

'I came to Twitter to find a quiet private place where I could put back the pieces of a self that felt broken and bruised in many places. To climb out of the dark hole in which I found myself. I could not be a mother to my children in this world. I did not know how to nurture myself and those I loved.'

'Words help me create a world that I can live in, that I do live in,' I replied.

The only way to begin to hear my voice was to walk towards the silence, I had tweeted one day.

Confidence is a paper plane. It soars, it crashes, I fold a new one.

I began to read everything Roger Ebert wrote. His ability to be present in the moment made him see in the movies what few others perceived. His prescience helped him read people and relationships both on and off screen with miraculous clarity. And he was not afraid of memories. He had the courage to let his memories hold his hand and take him back to see the movie of his life.

My children would recognize his Twitter profile photo and arrange their hands in front of their faces the same way. I sent him a photo of them mimicking him. He was so proud, he shared it on Twitter and his Facebook page.

Why do we extend ourselves? Because that is the meaning of life itself. Meeting another version of oneself and extending one's hand in support. It's the way to heal.

All this leftover love one feels, you want to give it away before it is too late. There is only one life and the survivor can never forget that again.

The news of Roger Ebert's death on 4 April, 2013, came to me in the form of condolences. Around the world, people stunned by the sudden loss reached out to each other, hoping for solace. Many people who had followed him and me, began to send me messages.

I read the words of Chaz Ebert, his wife, online. 'He looked at us, smiled, and passed away,' she had shared. 'No struggle, no pain, just a quiet dignified transition.'

Roger Ebert taught me to recognize and trust my voice. I learnt that no one is a stranger and inhibitions are just useless baggage.

'Roger Ebert strengthened my belief in God,' I tweeted. 'He lives in our spontaneous generosity, in love so strong, we wonder where it comes from.' In a second tweet I wrote: 'I know that will make you laugh out loud, @ebertchicago. Yeah, I said God and your name together.'

Roger Ebert was gone but I was still talking to him on Twitter. He might check his mentions. I think he will.

37

Our teachers live forever

'Think of your childhood,' he said to me. 'Think of the difficulties. How did you survive? How did you solve your problems?'

I thought to myself. I lied. Sometimes I stole. I cheated in school. My deep dark secret was that I was a bad child. I remembered the fantasies I'd narrate to friends. A family with a Russian lineage, an imaginary mother, friend, dog, even a VCR when we didn't have one. The lies to my parents about my life outside home and vice versa.

'I started reading. I found role models in books and comics, in *Reader's Digest* condensed anthologies,' I said.

Father Oswald Summerton was both my therapist and teacher. He knew the rest of the story. 'You are a born succeeder,' he said to me. 'You can innovate again.'

'SUCCEEDER.' I find this word written in capital letters in my notebook.

'We don't come here to get sympathy,' he would say. 'This is a training session for self-therapy. We come here to succeed. It's a bad parent that does not allow the child to enjoy her victories.'

I sighed as I sat down. I had taken a cab, dropped the children at my Mum's, nursed the baby one last time and then skidded in for a group therapy meeting.

'How are you doing today?' he said.

'Oh well,' I said. 'I'm the mother of three small children.'

'Have you read about the woman who had eight babies recently?'

'Oh yes,' I laughed. 'Octomom.'

Just like that. No more self-pity. A little laughter, some directed at oneself, some just a celebration. That I am here, we are here. All is well.

'Have you solved your problem?'

'No,' I said.

'Have you done your duty?'

'Yes,' I said.

'Then you have solved your problem,' he would say.

How could such simple words change my life? Why should this person care for me so deeply? I remember the love in his eyes when he listened to people I would have been impatient with.

Rebuild the child who may have been shattered in your childhood. The one who may not have been allowed to be herself. Make-believe the childhood that you wanted.

His patience put my faith back in me. His creativity made it seem so easy. He would cut through the smog of our pretensions, expectations and fears. My inner whirl would calm down.

'Maybe you like to feel bad,' he said one day.

'No, I don't,' I said.

'Kids sometimes like to feel bad so that they can go complaining and sobbing and get their share of Mummy. Think of why you would like to feel bad. What are you hoping to get?'

I knew whose attention I was desperate for.

'If I know him well enough,' said Father Os, referring to my husband, 'he will sprint in five seconds if he gets that impression.'

I laughed. 'Yes, he does!'

'Don't be a needy child and your partner won't be a rejecting parent with you. Don't try to please him and you won't resent him,' he said.

From these conversations, I learnt to say no without feeling guilty or deprived. Saying no to something else is a way of saying yes to more urgent, perhaps less visible, priorities.

I still had a few hours of uninterrupted work to do to meet a project deadline when the phone rang. Father Os, my greatest teacher, had died. I knew he had been ill. I had kept the next morning free to meet him.

I put the phone down. In my mind, I saw his face with his crinkly smile, his eyes shining at me. 'You know what you have to do,' he said with a tilt of his head. I put my feelings in a box and kept them aside. I stayed with work.

When the submissions were sent and the papers packed

away, I put my head down on my pillow and cried. I fell asleep. As soon as day broke, I went to meet him as I had planned. There were others, who had lived and worked with him. We hugged. I began to clean the meeting room. Chairs, diwans, bookshelves and noticeboards. The TV and DVDs. The spaces between the buttons on the TV remote.

I sat down on a chair and sobbed. When I opened my eyes again, there was a splash of morning light where he would have been sitting. I took a photo. Our best teachers can never leave us.

On my computer, I play back a video in which I am speaking at a memorial meeting in honour of Father Oswald Summerton. 'I would feel as if tight knots were becoming untied in me. It was like spreading the pieces of a large jigsaw puzzle on the floor. From memories, feelings, experiences and new perspectives, we would create a whole self. This is how I began to recover my ability to be loving towards the people I love.'

38

Islam Bo and the burden of innocence

Many hours had passed before I noticed that my gold ring studded with diamonds was missing from my finger.

'Oh hell,' I muttered to myself. 'What have I done?'

I was away from my husband's home in our village in east Uttar Pradesh and it would be hours before we would reach home again. I knew I had taken it off earlier in the morning and did have some idea of where I might find it if I was lucky.

When we returned home, it was midnight. I put our children to bed and went down to the kitchen to look inside the dustbin. I hoped to find the ring inside a crumpled page from a newspaper. But I didn't recognize any paper in the mess of the dustbin. I didn't tell anyone else because I didn't want to deal with other people's sense of alarm over a piece of jewellery that I had misplaced.

More importantly, I knew that it was best to keep this discreet because Islam Bo was involved. Islam Bo is a *naun* in our village—a woman who belongs to the caste of *nais*. Traditionally, the men from her community work as barbers. The women work in upper-class and caste homes as domestic help in the kitchen and give massages to women and newborn babies. They are also messengers in the village, and make announcements about marriages and birth and death rituals in the village. They own no farming land, are Muslim and poor.

I am a little bit in love with Islam Bo. She has the body language of a free child and is uninhibited in her expression, like a talented mime artist. This is a rare and refreshing trait in our traditional family home, where being proper and reticent are top virtues.

Islam Bo and I were the last two people to have seen my diamond ring. She had come to my room to give me an oil massage. We had spread a newspaper on the bed, to protect the bedcover. At some point when she was pressing my palms, I had removed my ring and kept it on the bed.

'Is it gold?' Islam Bo had asked.

'Yes,' I had said. 'And these are diamonds.'

She had said something in Bhojpuri in a scolding tone. 'Be careful, don't keep it so casually.'

I had forgotten to wear it again later and when I did not find it on my bed at night, I wondered if we had accidentally wrapped it in the newspaper and thrown it away.

I waited for Islam Bo to return the next day. She walked in carrying a fresh, organic paste of barley flour mixed with mustard oil and gestured to me from a distance that it was for me. I knew instantly that this woman was on my side.

In many ways, life in our village home is a window to the complex and intricate web of oppression and interdependencies that make up Indian society. I had known that if the news of my missing ring became public, it would spread quickly all the way to Islam Bo's home and she would stand accused of theft.

As soon as I confided in her that I had lost my ring, we began to trace the route of the crumpled newspaper from one dustbin to another. She overturned the garbage on to the earth and sifted through it with bare hands. We were in the open under a harsh sun. She was fasting for Ramzan. I got tired and lost hope and came back to my room. Twenty minutes later, Tarannum, who also works in the kitchen, came running to me with the ring. The ring my mother had gifted to me when my brother had got married. The ring, that despite my reassurances, had become Islam Bo's worst nightmare.

When I went out to thank and congratulate Islam Bo, she had tears in her eyes. I hugged her, held her hand and brought her to my room. She was overcome with emotion. I knew why. As a poor woman born in a low caste, she had repeatedly borne the burden of being suspected as guilty till she could produce the proof of her innocence. This is how our society is structured. This is how all of us participate in perpetuating inequalities.

Alone with me, Islam Bo began to tell me stories. I listened. She mentioned a guest from Lucknow who had misplaced her earrings and accused her of stealing them.

'People in this home who have known me for years said to me, "*Bura mat mano*" (don't feel bad). I said, if you say bad things to me, you can be sure that I will feel bad about it.'

'What is your name, Islam Bo?' I asked her after 15 years of knowing her. She is called Islam Bo because she is the wife of a man called Islam.

'Shareefun,' she said. 'But people have distorted it and everyone who uses the name says Shaleefun. Even my voter-ID card has my name as Shaleefun.'

'Why won't they say your name as it is?'

'We are poor,' she said. 'People get offended if we have good names. My daughters' names are Shaheena and Ruhi. But everyone calls them Mohfa and Tohfa. When Shaheena was born, your uncle was not even married, but when he gave his daughter the same name, we stopped calling our child by that name.'

As I do when I am unable to find words to express what I am feeling, I picked up my phone and took photographs of her. Shareefun has the widest grin in the world. I showed her the photograph I had taken.

'Delete it,' she said to me, looking cross. 'What is this face full of teeth showing? Let me pose properly. Take a photo without my teeth showing.'

When she rearranged her facial features for a proper photograph, Shareefun could not keep the sadness out of her eyes.

'Why so sad?' I said to her. She smiled for me. And pressed the pressure points on my palms and feet till I put my phone away and put my head back on the pillow.

'When you pray,' I said to my husband later, 'ask for an old age in which we have as much healing power in our hands as Islam Bo has in hers even on days when she is keeping her roza.'

'I don't need a lot of food,' Shareefun had said to me. 'Allah gives me strength. When I am tired, my granddaughter gives me a massage. I get okay again.'

39

A search turns into a metaphor

I did not immediately think of Rajni when I started planning my trip to Ambikapur. To be honest, I couldn't quite place Ambikapur in Chhattisgarh and had to find it on an online map.

My documentary film crew and I flew to Raipur and then took a night train to reach Ambikapur in Surguja district. As I left home, I had to strain to remember where I had written Rajni's address. I found it online on my blog. Rajni was from Jashpur district. I would be travelling to the district right next to hers. I had always wanted to meet Rajni in her own home.

Rajni Betila Tete was a therapist for me. Her presence kept me sane. After our second child was born and we moved out of our flat near my parents' home, we hired Rajni to stay and work in our new home in the suburb.

Both my husband and I would be away at work for

hours every weekday. Sometimes Rajni would accompany our children and me to the daycare facility at my office. Sometimes the toddler would stay at home with her, while the older child went to preschool.

Our household would swell and contract. We had friends, cousins, family and guests coming and staying with us regularly. Both my husband and I would travel for work. My life began to overwhelm me.

The first symptom that I recognized was my inability to handle weekends. I would sit somewhere and be unable to get up. I would fall ill and have stomach aches. I would look at Rajni for inspiration.

She had made some tough life choices. A tribal woman in her early 20s, she had come to Delhi as a migrant worker to be able to support her family in Chhattisgarh. Rajni showed me how to keep one's poise. She had a natural way of structuring her day that I didn't seem to have a knack for. There was a sense of self embedded in her erect spine that exuded strength.

She was happy. She was proud. She protected her boundaries.

Rajni had a special relationship with our toddler, Aliza. I worried about Rajni when we were not home and she would have to open the door to receive men. I worried about her when she went on long walks with the children. Rajni was single, beautiful, vulnerable in the city.

Every Sunday morning, Rajni went to a church at a convent school near our home. Sometimes she took Aliza with her. She would wear a sari and take the day off.

The last time she left our home, Rajni and I cried silently all the way to the railway station. There was a beauty in the letting go too. Rajni was going home. To her hills and forest. To her life as a farmer. Rajni had triumphed in her stint in the city.

I quit working in an office soon after Rajni stopped working in our home. Our lives were linked in that way. She went home and I came home. To have something to hold on to, I became obsessed with the idea of attending Rajni's wedding. I hate attending marriages. I have forsaken my best friends on their big day and found ways to be away when my closest cousins got married. But for some reason, I kept repeating to Rajni that we would come as a family to attend her wedding.

Rajni did not call us before she got married. She called me later one day when she was visiting her mother, and shared her happiness with me. She was shy on the phone.

That day in Surguja, I was a few kilometres away from Rajni's home. I did not know how to find her. Our shooting schedule was tight. Her mother's neighbour's mobile phone number has changed. Rajni hasn't called me recently. I consoled myself that the logistics of tracing her were too complicated.

I did not find my Rajni, but I found someone else whose story had me hooked. And we literally chased her across the town of Ambikapur.

'Have you noticed the autorickshaw drivers in Ambikapur?' Narendra had asked me on the second day of our shoot. Narendra works with a rights-based organization called Chaupal and was helping to organize the logistics of our shoot and interviews.

We drove past an autorickshaw stand and he pointed out a group of young women wearing khakhi coats over their salwar kameezes. Young tribal women driving autorickshaws in their own district headquarter. We began to follow an autorickshaw on the road that was being driven by a woman. Next to the number plate was her registration number, name and mobile number. Her name was Shosan Tirki.

I quickly went up to Shosan to ask for her permission to film her as she drove her passengers to their destination. She smiled and agreed. Shosan Tirki is barely 20 years old and now supports her family with her income. Her father is not well enough to work. At the autorickshaw stand, she introduced us to her colleagues. Women who looked young enough to be schoolgirls, twirling their autorickshaw keys and attending calls on their mobile phones. They were all parking their autorickshaws in a queue to attend a meeting called by the district collector, Ritu Sain.

Each one of them had the collector's mobile number stored in their phone. Each one of them seemed just like a younger version of Rajni. These women who would not have to travel to the metros as domestic workers because they had found and seized opportunities closer home.

We interviewed Sain, the district collector of Surguja, later in her home. 'My job is to give opportunities. Fair opportunities,' she said. 'Every woman I meet in the tribal communities living in forest areas as well as towns wants to work to better her circumstances. All I am doing is creating opportunity that is connected to the community and infrastructural needs that already exist. We are tapping into people's capabilities.'

Women in Surguja district are managing brick kilns, poultry and pig farms and fisheries. They are working as masons, parking lot attendants and canteen staff. They have formed self-help groups that produce and supply vegetables, hospital and school supplies, processed food, bricks and cement. It's a brave new world in Surguja.

In each one of these women, I saw a little bit of the Rajni who had supported me so well when I needed help. For now, my heart was full. I will find our real Rajni another time in this life.

40

Yet the heart remains troubled

After weeks of staying with us, it is time for my father-in-law to return to his home in his village in eastern Uttar Pradesh. We know what going home means to Papa. He belongs to his land, it sustains his breath and his sense of being. Mirza Ashfaq Beg is an important man there.

At the breakfast table, I cheerfully state the obvious. 'Papa, you are going home tomorrow!'

He pauses to look up and smile at me. Papa has a serious face but this smile that always reaches his eyes gives him away. He is easily amused and always ready to find humour in things. 'How are you feeling now, Papa?' I ask him.

'The doctors have given me a clean chit,' he says. 'But you know what they say...' He completes his sentence with an Urdu couplet:

Agar hal ho gayi mushkil to asaani nahi jaati,
Bahar soorat mere dil ki pareshani nahi jaati

(Even when all the problems seem to be solved, for some reason my heart still remains troubled.)

Last year, Papa was diagnosed with Parkinson's syndrome, and it was a great relief for all of us. I mean it was a relief for my husband and me, because the mystery of what had been happening to Papa over the last few years finally had an explanation. We had been concerned about Papa's slowing down and had been pushing him to walk more, to go out more, and generally snap out of what seemed like mild anxiety and depression. He would often miss a step while walking and one day he had fallen abruptly and suffered a fracture of the lower spine.

We didn't know if he would ever recover well enough to be independent again. The diagnosis gave us a name for the problem. Now we knew that Papa wasn't just being lethargic and absent-minded. He had a condition that was treatable. Collectively, we would beat it back.

Over the next few months, Papa recovered enough to move from his wheelchair to using a walker, and then just a walking stick. He travelled between his home and ours again and again. As we watch him interacting with his doctors, physiotherapists and caregivers, I realize he has a charm that is hard to describe. Doctors stop in the waiting area to ask about his well-being. They tell him they will be lucky to have his strength when they are as old as him. Despite their busy-ness, they chat with Papa about the mango season in Varanasi and the cool breeze of mango orchards.

I realize I am not the only one who loves to get his attention.

Sometimes I wake up extra chirpy and speak to my father-in-law as if I am a young girl all over again. This role-playing comes naturally to me, even though it has been decades since I've been like this with anyone. I remember girl friends in my college years, sometimes indulging me, sometimes asking me to switch off my face. Now it is my husband's turn to give me a side-eyed look. I ignore him. Papa responds to me with a quiet laughter. I often call him Papaji, in the Punjabi way that I was taught by my parents as a child.

I tell Papa about my work and travels. Like elderly parents tend to do, he wants all the details of logistics. Which route I am taking, who is going with me, who will receive me, where I will stay, when I will be back. He forgets most of the details, or maybe he asks again and again because he needs the reassurance.

He also makes sure that I am reassured of his approval. Again, he quotes poetry and leaves me with words to savour.

Sair kar duniya ki ghafil, zindagani phir kahaan,
Zindagi gar kuchch rahi, to naujawaani phir kahaan
(Travel this world, o ignorant one, because life is short.
Even if life lasts long enough, your youth won't come back again.)

I'm sitting next to him on his bed as I write down this couplet to remember it later. 'Won't you have breakfast, Mami?' asks my nephew. 'No,' I answer him, 'not until Papa is ready to join too.'

'She is making up for lost time,' says Papa with a smile. 'All the time she has been away while I was here.' Then he instructs his grandson to get a cup of tea for me.

More than ever before, my father-in-law feels like my grandfather to me. We discuss the news. I complain to him about things that get to me. 'You know how your son is...' I often start my sentences, when he asks me where he is or why he is later than expected. We share jokes about this man who is the reason behind our relationship with each other.

Often there will be some tension between father and son. The roles have been reversed between them and neither of them is comfortable with it. They both miss Ammi, who was the buffer between them. Papa has more grace than his son when a conflict arises. It is hard to watch, yet it is beautiful to witness. Despite the fragility of his physical self, there is a quiet strength that never betrays him.

It makes me think of how many times Papa has known defeat in this long life of his. How many times he has chosen peace over confrontation for the sake of the greater good.

He was 19 years old when India became independent in 1947. It was an exhilarating moment of collective victory, yet it was also a time of personal crisis for his family. His elder brother and his family were torn away from them over the next few years, as the borders between India and Pakistan became harder to cross. Papa got admission in Dhaka University's engineering course but homesickness brought him back to India.

'I couldn't eat rice all the time. I needed my *rotis*,' he smiles as he remembers that time.

'What would have happened if you had stayed in Dhaka?' I ask him.

He nods his head, gesturing a no. 'I was always with

Maulana Abul Kalam Azad. We were never in favour of the two-nation theory. The partition of India was a political stunt that went horribly wrong. It drove a wedge between communities that has never healed.'

I have many questions for Mirza Ashfaq Beg. I want to make sense of things that seem inexplicable, I want to understand why we didn't transform as we had expected to. Sometimes he answers me with anecdotes; sometimes he offers me the gift of poetry, reminding me that he is passing on the baton from one generation to the next.

VII

Becoming Me

I like this about growing up. You can live in many different decades of your own life simultaneously.

41

Are you large, do you contain multitudes?

'Mamma, children in my class ask me, if your father is a Muslim, what is your mother?'

This is not the first time that one of our daughters has brought this question home. It isn't just children who ask this question point blank either; grown-ups do too.

This time it was our middle child when she was in class VII, in a school she had joined the year before, so her peers and she were still discovering each other. Aliza didn't choose a private moment to share this with me. She suddenly spoke up, from a distance, in a new place among new people.

We were in my sister-in-law's home, staying with her for a few days to attend her daughter's wedding. At that moment, we were sitting in an open veranda, resting between glittering wedding functions and grand feasts. There were various friends of different members of the family, aunts and uncles, cousins, my children and I.

Not only is this a difficult question to answer in the presence of an inter-generational, inter-family and inter-religious group, it is not a question that has a one-word answer. My children know that their mother is hard to label because she is neither a practising Muslim nor a practising Hindu and she loves to enter churches and the Baha'i Temple with a book in hand and sit still for long hours. There is Islamic calligraphy and Buddhist thangka art on the walls and tabletops in our home and various little Ganeshas are perched on window sills. One of them is a brass dancing Ganesha in a Nataraja pose. Another is a miniature sandalwood idol. All of these are presents from friends.

More accurately, if you distil religion to its pure form, like I do for myself, then I am both a practising Muslim and a Hindu. And a Sikh. I just don't care for most of the rituals, except the fun, easy and necessary ones.

I pray a lot, and I find that everyday language works perfectly well when I need to speak to God above all Gods, a term I learnt from my teacher, Father Os, who was both a trained psychotherapist and a Jesuit priest. It may happen later in my life, but so far I am just not inspired by words from any religious texts, except the ones that come in the form of poetry or song, like most of the teachings of Sufi and other mystical saints.

'Burn worldly love, rub the ashes and make ink of it, make the heart the pen, the intellect the writer, write that which has no end or limit,' Guru Nanak is quoted in the *Guru Granth Sahib*.

I love gurdwaras, temples, churches and mosques, mostly during their silent hours. Some of them have ponds and fish, some have trees, some have an open sky and cool stone floors, deities with large, imploring eyes and brass bells that must be clinked. I connect to the aura in their spaces. I feel peace and solace.

But people rarely want to hear real answers, leave alone elaborate ones.

Often a question about identity is spoken as if it is a judgement in itself. Sometimes a question sounds like an accusation. It is fired to prove that any answer you give will be deemed wrong. Others are not necessarily curious about your version of your self. The question is more like an intangible boundary they draw around their own set of beliefs. They are threatened by realities beyond the ones they have allowed themselves to imagine.

When my daughter spoke up among grown-ups, perhaps she wanted to hear the open, public version of my answer. As I write here, I have replied to her even more forthrightly now. There is nothing awkward or uneasy in my words. I will not let the tone of the question affect the tone of my answer.

I want children to learn that they can invalidate the queries of others. We will not participate in the narrowing of possibilities; we will expand them. We create our own frames of reference and protect our boundaries. We speak clearly and with candidness.

I am reminded of words from Walt Whitman's *Song Of Myself*.

Do I contradict myself?

Very well then I contradict myself,

(I am large, I contain multitudes.)

'Mamma, children ask me how come your mother's name is Natasha Badhwar if your name is Aliza Beg.' This was the child's next salvo.

'Goodness gracious me,' I said. 'This one is easy. You just have to say—Hey, it's 2017, baby! Get on with the times. Next year just say it's 2018. Then 2019. Then after you have crossed 2020, you can say—just google me.'

I wanted to make her laugh. I wanted to relieve everyone around me of the false notion that children are confused or burdened by the idea of multiple identities. Children pick up stereotypes from the adult world, pausing to examine them as they grow up. We only pretend to protect our children from realities that we are ourselves unwilling to face up to.

'Mamma, can my name be Naseem Badhwar Beg?' our youngest child asked me later.

'If you would like it like that, of course it can,' I said.

'I would like it like that,' she said. 'It will be amazing.'

42

Call me by my name—All of them

I don't know what went through my father's mind when the elderly Irish nuns in the principal's office in Loreto Convent, Ranchi, suggested that he reconsider the name he had chosen for me. Apparently, I was too sweet a child to have such a common name.

I was four years old and my name was Neeru. I remember being flattered by the attention. To my eyes, these were powerful, authoritative, kindly women. My parents seemed intimidated by them. It was very important for them to get their child admitted to this prestigious convent school.

'What are your brothers' names?' the principal asked me.

'Nitish and Manish,' I answered.

'Would you like to be called Natasha or Manisha?'

There was already a Manisha in our neighbourhood. I didn't want her name. 'Natasha,' I answered. Just like that, I had a new name.

I had never felt anything amiss in this story about how I was renamed within minutes, on the whim of someone who was a stranger to us, till my English friend Dawn pointed it out to me when I was 19. I had been breezily repeating this anecdote whenever anyone asked me how I came to have a Russian name. 'I'm named after my brother actually,' I'd say. 'It was an Irish nun's idea.'

'How racist!' Dawn had exclaimed with disgust. 'How dare she suggest that your own name wasn't good enough for you?'

It took years for this to sink in. I spoke to my parents about it, but discussions about race, caste, class, structural inequalities and systemic discrimination are not my parents' most comfortable choices when talking to their children. They are both first-generation graduates in their respective families, and for them it is an achievement to have found their feet in the fast pace of urban India. They did whatever was required of them to give us access to every opportunity they could afford for us.

My mother had chosen the name Neeru for me, inspired by the character of a 'very good girl' in a story she had read in a Hindi magazine called *Sarita*. My earliest memories confirm that I had no plans of becoming the kind of obedient girl that Sudha, my mother, had imagined. Over the years, I would disappoint her repeatedly and in many different ways. I would also make Sudha proud in unexpected ways. For her, I have always remained Neeru. My own brand of Neeru.

Although he had not resisted the renaming of his

daughter in the room in which it took place, my father had intervened in his own way. When we moved to Kolkata, he changed the spelling of my name to Nitasha when he was enrolling me in a new school. It felt like an Indian name to him now. His name for me.

This time he had to deal with my quiet rebellion. I changed the spelling back to Natasha when we moved to Delhi and I was in yet another new school. I didn't want an Indian-sounding name. I preferred the authentic version, the one that I found in Russian films that we watched on Doordarshan, and in my father's copy of Leo Tolstoy's *War And Peace*.

By the time I left school, I had begun to rebel against my second name—Badhwar. Every time I filled a new application form, I would try to get away with not using the second name. I would write my mother's name instead of my father's name wherever I could manage. My Delhi Transport Corporation bus pass, my British Council and American Library membership cards, even my Provident Fund forms, when I first started working, had just my first name on them. I was trying to fix something that seemed dissonant to me.

When friends asked me about it, I'd say: 'My family is looking forward so keenly to seeing me married and losing this name, I thought I'd just lose it anyway. Problem solved.'

My husband noticed that I had begun to use Badhwar more often after we got married. Sometimes, when I speak aloud to myself these days, I often call myself Badhwar. For example: Stop being distracted, Badhwar or Aren't you a good girl, Badhwar?

Unlike my parents and me, Afzal doesn't leave any of his thoughts unspoken. 'How come you have become a Badhwar since you have been living with me?' he has asked me on more than one occasion, not satisfied with any of my replies. 'You used to insist that you are "just Natasha" earlier.'

Mostly, I smile in reply, letting him know that I may or may not know the answer to this. If I feel that an identity is being thrust on me, I may not allow it to stick. If I feel that it is being threatened, I may wrap it more snugly around myself. Maybe I've just become used to seeing both names together in print and on my Facebook profile. They seem like one name now. Maybe I am bigger, and I need to use my bigger name. Who knows?

Our youngest child brought up the topic of names recently. 'Mamma, can my name be Naseem Badhwar Beg?' she asked me, sitting at the dining table after she had returned from school. She has asked this before, but we have not formalized it yet.

'Do you want it to be?' I asked her.

'Yes, Mamma,' she said. 'I want the full family name.'

I may have thought it was cool to drop my father's name as a feeble protest against patriarchy, but for my child it is her mother's name, and she wants it included in her own formal name. It feels ironic and sweet and reminds me of the circle of life all over again.

43

Running to catch up with the forties

The only thing I really want and don't have is the perfect pair of spectacles, I think to myself on a good day. The technology of progressive lenses has failed me. Or it could be that my eye muscles are still strong enough and do a better job than overpriced spectacle lenses.

I have consistently been a late adopter. My gadgets are usually one or two generations behind. Even if a benefactor buys me the newest tech in the market, I will often let it lie unopened in its fancy box for a couple of years. I did this with my first iPhone and now I am treating our Google Home device the same way.

Perhaps because of this slowness, this desire to go deep rather than forward, I become absent-minded and forget to move at the same pace as my age. It took me a long time to become 40, even after I had turned 40. Now I worry the 40s will race away before I have had enough of them.

'Eat walnuts,' a friend messaged in response to my lament that my short-term memory has gone missing. I ordered them online but when I ate them dutifully, the walnuts reminded me that I need to upgrade the fillings in my molars.

I love my dentist and after a few successful root canal treatments in the last decade, I have been worrying about how I will get to meet her again. Thanks to the walnuts, I have an appointment with her once again. There are some happy endings after all.

In my mid-40s, I have discovered that anyone's life can be a situational comedy, provided one learns to look for the laughs in unexpected places.

Sometimes when I visit my parents, I go back to the market where we used to hang out as young adults. Often I will spot a face and strain to recognize him, till I realize that these familiar-looking boys are grown sons of the dashing fellows who used to swagger late to our U-special bus-stop. Those promising blokes who used to call themselves DJ, Yanks and Sam are now being annoying uncles on the RWA WhatsApp group.

'Walk barefoot on grass every day,' another friend advised when we reconnected. We were meeting after years and for some reason we kept exchanging notes on our diet restrictions and exercise routines. Then we shared updates on her cat and my daughters. All the while we were talking about urgent things of the present, in my mind I was actually going back to the books, music and artists we had discovered together. I really was having a parallel conversation with her in my own head.

I like this about growing up. You can live in many different decades of your own life simultaneously. You still don't know what's ahead but there is such rich material to work with from the life you have already lived.

Sometimes there is so little time to catch up with friends that one has to stick to the very basics. With many friends, if there's time for only one question, then that has become, 'Is your Mum okay? How is your father doing?'

'Yes, she's good, she may need surgery but she's safe. What about your parents?' asks your friend. And you give a thumbs-up sign because your time is up and you will have that much-awaited in-depth conversation later.

I used to think that it was only a matter of time and practice before I would find my voice and learn to speak up where I had stayed silent earlier. Yet I find I am quieter than ever before. I need to speak even less. Why rise to an ill-intentioned bait at all? The arguments that deserve to be battled with are not in our drawing rooms anyway. They are outside our comfort zones.

Spontaneity. I am happy to report that despite years of self-training to keep it down, it hasn't become lethargic from disuse. In fact, it retains its enthusiasm for startling people when they aren't quite ready for it. I am restoring spontaneity to my armour.

I still feel shy when I make a new friend. It is most annoying because being confident and shy at the same time confuses me too.

I continue to learn from people like I did when I was 20. I identify mentors and watch them as if my brain is mapping the blueprint of theirs, making notes of their reactions, poise and charm.

I have figured out net banking. I still give grief to my stoic chartered accountant over the filing of tax returns. My reading list is longer than ever before. The list of things I will do after I complete this two-year-long list of things to do right now, continues to be ambitious.

I still haven't succumbed to the temptation to write off people. I have given up on arguments without bothering to engage. But I am holding on to the belief that people are more than what they say they believe. It's a waste of time to take them personally.

My enthusiasm for other people's weddings is at its all-time low. I hear of my own cousin's impending wedding and wonder what it will take to avoid attending it. Maybe I need to win an international award that will keep me out of the country in that exact week. There's hardly ever enough lead time to start and finish the work that may culminate with a must-attend award ceremony. So my advice to you guys is to be consistent if you want to have great excuses to avoid family weddings. Work hard. Have a vision. Otherwise, one will just have to break a leg. Or two.

My enthusiasm for new babies being born is at an all-time high. I had lost interest in other people's infants and toddlers but now I am dangerously close to wanting to kidnap one of them again. 'Let's get a dog,' my children try to distract me. But I am afraid of falling in love with a higher life form and becoming unavailable to the current ones who need me.

I have become better than before at attending funerals, although there is no logic yet in how I may react when news of another death arrives. I can cry for days at home, and still not be able to call the friend who has lost the parent or sibling. This helps neither the friend nor the ones who have to deal with me at home. I apologize for my imperfections.

I'm rebellious about milestones imposed on me and I encourage you to neglect them too. Being absent from where you are supposed to be means you are present somewhere else.

Once you give yourself the permission to be available only where you choose to be, you can have a lot of secret fun. And that really is the freshest ingredient behind twinkling eyes and a spring in one's step.

44

My body is a photographer

'Who are the technophobes in this class?' asked Shohini Ghosh on the first day when Sabeena Gadihoke and she were to begin the practical demonstration of video cameras to our class of postgraduate mass communications students.

My hand shot up like a Diwali rocket. Finally a question I could answer like an expert. I wanted to be the first to be noticed. My eagerness was unnecessary because my hand remained the only one raised in class.

'Good,' said Ghosh. 'That's the next Steven Spielberg amongst us.'

I was stunned. I was expecting to be lectured, perhaps even mocked. I had been flaunting my I-am-petrified-of-technology identity as if it were a badge of honour. It kept me safe from being judged for my performance if I leapt to the first position in the queue for losers voluntarily.

Spielberg's *Jurassic Park* was still fresh in our minds. We had all celebrated E.T. the Extra-Terrestrial as teenagers. He was the greatest science-fiction director we knew in the mid-1990s.

Just like that, without much forethought or planning, I received a kind of psychic permission from my teachers. I usually tried to stay invisible in class. I hardly engaged in discussions and media theory and politics left me numb at that age. Ghosh would have said what she said to whoever raised his or her hand.

Her repartee was so unexpected that it knocked the smugness out of me. When the film and video cameras were introduced to us, I hovered around them tentatively. The first time we went out to film visual sequences, I realized that there is a machine that is made for me. Cameras listened to me. Together we created meaning. A new language had come to me, just like that.

I loved the physicality of the process of shooting. Using my hands and my body to create. Not having to be pretty or graceful for anyone else's gaze. Getting dirty and dusty, getting real. It is both my yoga and my meditation.

For someone with poor social skills and a voice that often failed me, the camera became my primary tool of expression. With a 13 kg camera balanced on my shoulder, one eye shut and the other looking through the viewfinder, I became a complete person. I could tell stories now.

When it was time to choose professional roles in the media industry, seven of my classmates chose to be camerapersons. Three of us were women.

It took me more than a year to get fully familiar with the video camera, its parts and functions, and its technology. I carried a checklist in my pocket for a long time to reassure myself. I borrowed tapes from the video-tape library and watched raw footage shot by seniors whose work I admired. I volunteered for double shifts and made myself available at work at all hours. I was hungry for opportunity and experience. I wanted to connect to beauty and humanity.

Being on location, taking flights, sleeping on trains and driving through mountain roads with the video camera in my lap became home for me. Every day I challenged myself to compose at least one new shot I had never taken before.

Becoming a cameraperson unlocked my inner teacher. I could teach anyone who wanted to learn how to be a visual storyteller. And I did. My best students learnt nothing from me. All I did for them was what my teachers had done for me. I took away their fears and inhibition from them so they were liberated enough to see the light. I gave them permission to express themselves in their own unique way and pace.

My cameras and I witnessed death and despair together. We saw poverty and injustice. We met people with iron wills. We reassured and inspired others. We soaked in sunsets. We became friends. We made judgements and took decisions. We sweated and smiled together. We transported stories from one to many every day.

When I was tired and depleted, I took time off. When I became a mother, I put down my cameras. I didn't have enough hands. I needed to hold and be with the babies. I thought it was over between cameras and me.

I remember crying real tears. My daughters will never know who I used to be, I thought. I was silly. Whatever made me feel that I would never recover my former self was wrong and toxic.

When I quit my job at a broadcast station, I didn't even have a camera any longer. I thought I would never be strong enough again.

I went into the garden with my phone's VGA camera. I found myself creating images that even I could not see with my naked eye. My body had become a camera. It responded to how the light was falling. My knees, spine and hands knew how to bend and contort to find compositions.

Images saved me again. Images speak to me. I speak via images. For many years I spoke, not in words, but pictures. I needed the silence to recover my tongue. I needed the fog to wipe clean the dissonance.

Who am I to tell the story of others, I had felt, when it came to using words. I wasn't even ready to tell my own. I didn't trust my words. I told stories in pictures. Frames, compositions, light playing favourites and leading me to the details of people's lives.

That time when I felt painfully fragmented in my life, I began to put together the pieces of my own self with photos. No one was looking at me. I began to see me. Under the layers of isolation and silence, there was my inner child. Light from the bathroom window reflecting off the white wall and becoming a twinkle in my eye. I brought myself back into existence with photos.

I am a photographer. I can say this with certainty. I do not feel like an imposter when I use this word for myself. My body is a photographer.

45

Discover the India within you

I had never been hungry in my life before. I was living in a tribal hamlet called Khodamba, which was a day's travel away from the town of Alirajpur in Madhya Pradesh. After a 6-hour bus ride through a dusty landscape of barren brown hills, we would trek for 3 hours through a hilly forest to reach Khodamba. This village of Bhil tribals was a cosy bowl-shaped clearing in the forest, with fields in the centre and homes dotted on the gentle slopes of the hills around it.

Some evenings I would watch the setting sun and smoke rising from kitchens in the distance and feel that it looked close to the photos of Switzerland I had seen on calendars in homes. Many afternoons I would go behind a mango tree, hold myself in a hug and cry till I felt lighter.

I was 21 years old and had volunteered as a teacher in an ongoing education project for tribal children. My diary entries from those days are desperate, often featuring tears and laced with self-deprecating humour. I was obsessed with my hunger, the heat, the lack of water, the lice in my hair and my struggle to socialize with the people I had come to live and work with.

'Did I fight with my family and come this far to do what I want to do only to discover that I am no good at this,' I wrote in my diary. I felt like a complete failure.

A typical day would start at 5 am and I would be called for the first meal only by 11 am. One large thick roti made of cornflour and a portion of watery dal. My eyes would follow the children who flitted in and out of the kitchen, picking up pieces of leftover rotis. It was mango season but the rains had failed and the trees bore no fruit that year.

'I have never been hungry before I came here,' I said to astonished people. I dreamt of food in vivid colours.

I abandoned the teaching project midway to join a postgraduate course in mass communications in Delhi. It had become the biggest conflict ever between my parents and me. I wanted to defer my admission and stick it out in the village. My parents could not imagine throwing away an opportunity that their peers told them was rare.

A year later, I went back to Khodamba with a classmate to film my first student project. I discovered that I did have a deep relationship with the village and people who had hosted me.

Despite that, I internalized a dark sense of failure, of having broken a promise and betrayed a dream. I judged myself severely for many years. I imagined that my mentors were disappointed in me. Looking back, I realize I had set my expectations too high too soon. I was used to being a high achiever and my stint in the tribal village had revealed my limitations to me.

I carried a burden that overwhelmed me secretly, paralysing me further as I made career and personal choices over the years. I had felt isolated in the village and now I felt isolated inside my mind.

I had believed that the way to live a more just and honest life was to abandon my privilege. I learnt that privilege is impossibly tenacious. The more I try to negate it, the more it grows. I can spend three months in a drought-affected area, living below the poverty line, and tell stories about it for three decades. It earns me easy admiration. It helps me qualify for prestigious courses, jobs and awards. I get to write think pieces in newspapers.

The only way to address this conflict was to embrace it. It has taken me years, even decades, to be able to process it. How can I contribute to the greater good in a sustainable way?

I learnt to look at the privilege of my birth as the well that will never stop giving. Throwing rocks and mud into it and trying to destroy what I can take from it is a fallacious choice. Recognize your power and put it to work. Be good at whatever you do. Infuse your sensitivity in every choice you make. Live more justly, pay more equitably, allow yourself to fail again and again. Your safety nets are too secure.

Put your guilt to work. Give your wallowing self some real targets to achieve. Success is a drug, have the conviction to detox and step back. If your pain is real, it will choose to heal.

My career as a video journalist and documentary film-maker took me back into other people's homes again and again. We constantly needed others to extend themselves so that our work could get done. It is easy to forget their generous contributions to our work and take all the credit for 'my story,' 'my shots,' 'my film' and 'my breaking news'.

We already know how to manipulate narratives. We know when to dip into others' lives, take what we want and when to disconnect. It is easy to thrust heroism upon ourselves, even more so now that we have social media at our fingertips.

Acknowledge this mindfully to pierce through your own complacency.

Looking back, I realize that again and again I have intuitively chosen experiences that challenge my abilities and often break me temporarily. Every time I travel away from comfort, I come face to face with my own conscience. I realize how little I know and how wrong my assumptions are.

What I look for is a way to know and connect with the India around me. Complex, diverse, energetic India. The India that hurts.

Somewhere this is connected with the desire to belong. To find home. Home isn't where one is pampered and safe. I feel incomplete and alienated in worlds that are padded with luxury and privilege. I want to know my worth. I want to know what I can affect with my power and presence as an individual.

We don't necessarily have to travel to the deep interiors of society to address injustice. We do, however, have to travel into the depths of our own consciousness. Each person reading this sentence has the power to change lives, to live more equitably, to participate in the information economy more responsibly.

Travel to the India within yourself. Connect to the India around you, the communities your life intersects with. Our personal lives are deeply political. We participate in perpetuating class, caste and gender inequality every day. Instead of obsessing with what you cannot do, focus on what you can enable.

Amplify what needs attention, smash your fist through paralysing ennui. When I stopped mocking and judging myself, I found the energy to put my strengths to use. I no longer try to simplify the world around me into problems and solutions.

We replenish our own life force when we connect to those of others. We can do no good for anyone else unless we acknowledge the good it does to us.

46

Why I hate writing

I hate writing because writing makes me a better person. Sometimes writing brings in help. I don't like asking for help. Yet, I often don't realize that I am sending out an SOS message calling for help when I allow my stream of consciousness to go for publishing.

When I wrote about Jyoti Devi, the 12-year-old schoolgirl in Hamirpur, Uttar Pradesh, who had only read one pamphlet besides her school books, I did not know that so many people would write in and offer books for her schoolmates and her. In retrospect, that must have been the only reason why I chose that one conversation to start the article on her. Within a week of publication, cartons of children's books were being couriered to a village in Uttar Pradesh to create a library in a government-run primary school. People read the story of bright children and their aspirations and were moved to act. To share their privilege with others.

Writing connects the stories. The writing brain is usually not the social self. It is slower and smarter. Writing forces me to understand and unravel, rather than judge.

Write long enough and one begins to see one's reflection on the page. As if the light has shifted and transformed the screen into a mirror. Writing reveals us to ourselves.

All writing is letter-writing. Writing is a conversation. For the longest time, I had no idea who I was writing to. The answers began to reveal themselves years later. Sometimes I go on writing on something long after I have submitted the word limit I am allowed.

Writing slows me down. It makes me confront my confusion and lack of clarity. Writing humbles me.

When I start anew, I realize that I cannot really write much when I try to write. I have to find ways to reach that desperate place where my conscious, thinking mind becomes silent and the words begin to arrive in their own rhythm and for their own reasons. I have to mute the self that speaks and thinks all the time and let stories emerge from an unfamiliar space, almost like music. I have to deliberately make this act un-deliberate and then it works.

Writing releases angst. Writing is the beginning of brave. It confronts cowardice. It shakes up lethargy.

Sometimes I write because I need to spit. Anger and disgust boils over. I was in a village, visiting family a few years ago. A 16-year-old girl in the neighbourhood had refused to go back to her marital home after she returned to her parents' home for the first time since she had been married. The groom was in his 50s.

'She has been watching too many TV serials,' someone commented. There was apathy all around. Malice and voyeurism.

Writing helped me climb out of the darkness of the dry well I seemed to have plunged into. It banished helplessness and brought back the awareness of my power and privilege. My responsibility.

Writing gives us permission. It restores our shattered self. It shames and inspires us to act. It brings validation. Writing is sharing—both our strengths and vulnerabilities.

Writing makes us read better. I scour words by others, looking for sentences that say what I have also felt. I look for worlds that are more honest than the one I am stuck in. I am forced to become honest to deserve entry into a better world.

Writing takes less time than reading. It is harder, but reading eventually leads to us beginning to write. Writing eventually makes us alive again.

Writing makes me join the world. It breaks down walls and opens the windows. Writing un-isolates me.

For some people, running is writing. Drawing is writing. So is singing. Sometimes sleeping is writing. Dreams are blog posts.

Writing can be a pious activity, like a prayer after a bath. It has to be done with a clean and honest intent. Its purpose is to focus our own mind so we can draw on our abilities.

Writing repairs love. It replenishes what is run down from overuse and neglect. It gives us a way to express what we otherwise are too wound-up to say.

Our language lies unused when we don't write. Untold stories make us restless and hyperactive.

I hate writing like I hate sitting down to meditate. It calms down the angsty child and transfers energy to the playful one. It restores order and power, creating connections that heal.

47

So tell me what makes you cry

I am sitting near the finish line of a school sports day function. I am crying. Cannot stop the tears. I take out my dark glasses and wear them to camouflage my expression.

I am surprised at myself. I was trying to avoid the sun, ready to be bored in a while, when I saw a tall, lean pre-teen girl make that final dash towards the end of a 200 m race to make it to the third position.

My tears started flowing. Something about children pushing themselves to do their best. They are in the moment. They are pushing their boundaries, creating something anew of themselves.

I clap for all the children, especially the ones who finished last. After all, they made it through the heats. They are all good at being themselves, they are all special. My palms are red. I wipe my snotty nose.

We forget how much there is in each individual child. We forget our own capabilities and dreams.

Now there is a judo demonstration after the athletic events are over. This girl with the high ponytail who is both a classical dancer and a judo champion. The determination on her face. Her grace and power.

It is time for the medals to be awarded. The serious-faced school trustee is smiling at each child today. Love, innocence, courage, endurance—when we witness them in their purer form, it moves the tectonic plates inside us. We feel something in our skin and bones. It reminds us of a version of us that we have been neglecting.

I have to get up and leave early. I have work to do. Presentations to deliver. I try to switch off my mind. Or my heart. Call it what you will.

I cried a lot before writing all this. I cried for years, often at places where it was inappropriate. I risked ridicule and smudged eye make-up to get to this moment at which I can blow my nose and start typing.

It's okay, it was mainly for research purposes. If I wanted to analyse various types of breads or kebabs, I would have to sample them before I would be able to write about them. Just like that, I had to cry a lot to get here.

My grandfather's sister was from Faridkot in Punjab and often came and stayed with us in Delhi. Buaji was loving and hilarious. We were at the wedding of my mother's niece and had reached the final part, the *bidai*, when the bride leaves with the groom in a flower-bedecked car. It was a sunny Sunday afternoon, there were jokes and laughter, but our Buaji was weeping loudly.

I remember being embarrassed and flummoxed. She wasn't even related to the bride.

'Why are you crying, Buaji?' I asked her. 'No one cries like this anymore.' She was inconsolable. I wondered who she was crying for.

I have become my elderly Buaji much sooner than I could have predicted. I cry at the weddings of strangers and I cry at the sight of children playing under flyovers at traffic lights. I cry when people tell stories they have saved up to tell for years.

I attend a lot of school functions. I always forget how much I am going to cry when children begin performing on stage. I never have a handkerchief or tissues. I am often wearing kaajal. Memories are triggered. The serious expressions on the faces of performers. The joy and determination of the dancers as they keep pace with the choreography. The tabla players, the actors in the background, little people searching for their parents in the direction of the audience. What is on their mind?

It is easy to cry in the darkness of the auditorium. I have also been crying in gurdwaras. In broad daylight. I crave to sit in a corner and hear gurbani being sung. I don't go up to the altar and bow like I have been taught to. I sit and listen to the prayers and try to figure out who I am mourning for.

Both my grandmothers had died before I was nine. I was too young and far away to mourn for them. They come in my dreams now and tell me their stories. My nani was living on an island and listening to the music of the band Indian Ocean in my dream. She told me that she had survived. She was happy. My dadi was a fish in a temple lake. She asked me to look out for her son, my father.

Admitting my despair makes me cry. My tears wash away the delusion that the world my daughters are growing up in is better or fairer than the one I grew up in. Crying makes me let go. Put down the baggage I am dragging around with me.

Bad news makes me numb. It is when the good news arrives that I break down and cry. By then, the more rational ones ask, 'Why are you crying now?'

I met a group of my students after 15 years and my tears began to queue up right behind my wide smile. Was I crying for who I once was? Crying because they had all done so well? Crying because of the nagging fear that perhaps I could have done better for them? You are being self-indulgent, I chided myself.

'What are you writing about?' my brother texted me this morning.

'Tears,' I wrote back.

'Real or artificial,' he asked.

'Inexplicable tears,' I answered. 'When we cry but don't understand why the hell we are crying.'

I wasn't expecting him to respond. I have never known Bhai to cry. He has always been stoic.

'I do it too these days,' he wrote back. 'I cry when I am driving. It makes me feel better, and then I play music at full volume in my car. *Tu kisi rail si guzarti hai...*'

'That's nice to hear,' I said.

'Nobody teaches you this. It is better to let our children see the truth now than try to figure it out in their 40s. Let them see our attempts to be a better person.'

I sent him an emoticon. Twelve hours separate his time zone from mine.

'Don't be ashamed and don't do it forever,' he wrote back.

I stayed calm in the virtual chat window. In real life, I was filled with joy. My brother has been crying. He is hurting and healing.

So tell me what makes you cry?

Why I decided to write my fears

I find it amusing to come face to face with my fears because I take myself pretty seriously as a grown-up and grown-ups are not supposed to have childish fears.

Right?

Yet, fears are so tenacious. You think you are done with them, you have gained confidence and experience, and then suddenly you are about to do something you have done many times before and you realize that you are engulfed with vague feelings of dread all over again.

Are they original? No. Are they universal? Probably. Are they real or are they foolish? Both.

Sometimes, if we surprise our fears by naming them, they themselves feel too sheepish to stick around.

In the first chapter of this book, I was making a list of my anxieties around writing these essays. I was whining because writing about being a parent to young children would mean that I would have to be more self-aware. I would have to be more present. To be able to write anything worth reading, I would have to be honest. To be honest, I would have to be good, and it feels so wasteful to be a responsible adult when no one significant is watching.

Being decent is hard work but over time we find out that it sure beats being indolent and decadent. Plus it is much more awkward to be nasty and then have to be honest about it.

As I continued to write these essays over the years, I really wanted to make them work. To be useful, somehow. I needed to hear from readers and peers to guide me, and that happened effortlessly. It still feels foolish and inappropriate to share about one's inner life in this external way, but my sharing has catalysed others. Sometimes there is mocking and rejection, but the engagement from readers continues to make me believe that even if I cannot always articulate the motivation behind personal writing, I must not doubt its relevance.

Not everything can be spoken in words. Therefore we write. We create.

What I didn't expect was that I really would become better understood. The initial feedback was always from readers I did not know personally and for years I remained worried about embarrassing and offending those closest to me—my family, friends and other inconvenient relatives.

There is, however, a great power in perseverance. In sticking it out even when one wonders whether one is moving forward at all or not. After about a decade of writing, I find that all these words have changed me and the world I live in. My mother gets me, my brother trusts me, my husband protects me and my children and father are mildly proud of me. I accept myself better. I smile at myself in the bathroom mirror as if it is natural to smile at oneself.

Stories trick us. A story that starts off looking like it's my story turns out later to be everyone else's story.

‘Snatching the eternal out of the desperately fleeting is the great magic trick of human existence.’

—Tennessee Williams

In Gratitude

There are many beginnings to this book.

I'll start with thanking Rahul Srivastava, who made this book possible in an inspired moment of intuitive decision-making. One minute we were finalizing my first book contract with Simon & Schuster India for *My Daughters' Mum*, and within minutes Rahul suggested, 'Why don't we do a 2 book contract right away?'

So we did. And that's how *Immortal for a Moment* was first imagined as a companion book along with *My Daughters' Mum*.

This book also started when Priya Ramani first commissioned the column, *My Daughters' Mum* in *Mint Lounge*, the weekend supplement of *Mint*, the financial daily newspaper published by HT Media. As an editor, Priya seemed so confident of what would emerge, that it often felt like she wasn't even looking at the columns I filed.

As the Editorial Director at Simon and Schuster India who commissioned the two books, Dharini Bhaskar gave new life to all the words. She saw light and connections in my work when I felt blinded by my proximity to it. Dharini will always remain my guardian angel.

My deep, heartfelt gratitude to Himanjali Sankar who inherited me when she joined Simon & Schuster as the next Editorial Director and stood by me gently and with great humour as I swung from over-confidence to abject self-doubt. Himanjali has been a friend, partner and guide in the journey of making this book a reality.

My gratitude to Anindita Ghose and Sanjukta Sharma, my editors at *Mint Lounge*. Like a sponge, I absorb learnings from you.

I thank Sayantan Ghosh for his eagle-eyed editing skills, his inspired Twitter feed and the encouragement and support he offers with just a wide smile.

Bharti Taneja from the marketing and publicity department is simply an author's best friend. She is full of ideas and stories and has made the post-book journey a breeze. Abhay Singh for his creativity and his polite approval of my creative ideas.

Richie Maheshwary, Head of Sales, for your stoic and clear-headed enthusiasm for taking our books to new places.

Sanket Jadia deserves a deep bow for his artistic skills and attention to detail in the design of this cover. Every iteration he presented was so attractive that it was hard to choose this final one.

Now for all my friends who have been my family in this lifetime. I am looking forward to how they will complain to me about the order in which their names appear here: Anshuman Mahaley, Geet Oberoi, Helen Vaid, Dawn Storey, Rachana Pandey, Shefali Bhushan, Radhika Bordia, Aparna Roy, Madhulika Mathur, Susmita Choudhuri,

Anupama Chandra, Manisha Mudgal, Paromita Vohra, Aneela Babar, Anu Singh Choudhary, Swastika Mehta, Dushyant, Mudrika and all my other secret loves.

My sister-in-law Sheetal Badhwar and her wonderful children, Madhav, Janki and Aditi make my world go around. Also my nephews and nieces–Mannat, Ananti, Nimit, Aiman, Areeka and my most special niece, Shireen.

Kanta and Ashok Bhati deserve a special mention for managing all the logistics of my life with love, patience and acceptance.

My parents, my brothers, my husband and children all get to be in one sentence. You are all my favourites, you know that.

Finally my readers, my true champions. Thank you for the attention and the generosity. It has brought me back to life.

Anupama Chandra, Manisha Mudgal, Paromita Vohra, Aneela Babar, Anu Singh Choudhury, Swastika Mehta Dushyant, Mudrika and all my other secret loves.

My sister-in-law, Sheetal Badhwar and her wonderful children, Madhav, Janki and Aditi make my world go around. Also my nephews and nieces–Mannat, Amrita, Nimit, Armaan, Aneeka and my most special niece, Shreem.

Kapo and Ashok Bhaiya deserve a special mention for managing all the vagaries of my life with love, patience and acceptance.

My parents, my brothers, my husband and children all get to be in one sentence. You are all my favourites, you know that.

Finally my readers, my true champions. Thank you for the attention and the generosity. It has brought me back to life.

Priyanka Parashar/Mint

Natasha Badhwar was born in Ranchi, grew up in Kolkata and refused to accept Delhi as home for the next three decades.

She is the author of *My Daughters' Mum—A book of permissions to love, laugh, heal and find one's way home*, adapted from her popular column 'My Daughters' Mum' in *Mint Lounge*. Along with Harsh Mander and John Dayal, she has co-edited the book, *Reconciliation–Karwan e Mohabbat's Journey of Solidarity through a Wounded India*.

Natasha began her career in broadcast journalism with New Delhi Television (NDTV) as the first female videographer in news television in India. She quit thirteen years later as vice president, training and development. She now works as an independent film-maker, media trainer and columnist. She is a member of the Karwan e Mohabbat, a citizen's initiative that seeks justice and livelihoods for victims of hate crimes across India.

She lives in New Delhi with her husband and three daughters.

If you liked this book, you will love ...